AF540851

People's Linguistic Survey of India

Volume Twenty-Three, Part II

THE LANGUAGES OF PUDUCHERRY

People's Linguistic Survey of India

Volume Twenty-Three, Part II

THE LANGUAGES OF PUDUCHERRY

Chief Editor

G. N. Devy

Editors

L. Ramamoorthy

G. Ravisankar

Orient BlackSwan

THE LANGUAGES OF PUDUCHERRY

ORIENT BLACKSWAN PRIVATE LIMITED

Registered Office
3-6-752 Himayatnagar, Hyderabad 500 029 (Telangana), India
e-mail: centraloffice@orientblackswan.com

Other Offices
Bengaluru, Bhopal, Chennai, Ernakulam, Guwahati,
Hyderabad, Jaipur, Kolkata, Lucknow, Mumbai,
New Delhi, Noida, Patna, Vijayawada

Volume Twenty-Three, Part II

First published by Orient Blackswan 2016

ISBN 978-81-250-6248-6

Maps by
Sangam Books (India) Private Limited
Hyderabad

Typeset by
Macrocom Enterprises, New Delhi
in Times New Roman 10.5/12.6

Printed at
Glorious Printers
Delhi

022843

04032016

Published by
Orient Blackswan Private Limited
1/24 Asaf Ali Road
New Delhi 110 002
e-mail: delhi@orientblackswan.com

The People's Linguistic Survey of India is a project of Bhasha Research and Publication Centre, partly funded by the Sir Jamsetji Tata Trust, Mumbai.

Contents

List of tables and figures

The People's Linguistic Survey of India

What is the People's Linguistic Survey of India?

The People's Linguistic Survey of India is a rights-based movement for carrying out a nation-wide survey to identify, document and understand the state of Indian languages, especially languages of fragile nomadic, coastal, island and forest communities.

The PLSI has been carried out by scholars, writers and activists in partnership with members of different speech communities.

It is a quick, non-hierarchical, public consultation and appraisal, intended as an aid to cultural impact assessment of development, and as an acknowledgement of the self-respect and sense of identity of all, especially the endangered speech communities of India. The PLSI is guided by the National Editorial Collective, constituted voluntarily.

The main objectives of the PLSI are

- To provide an overview of the living languages of India as 'they are' by 2011–2012.
- To create an action network of members committed to sustainable development, irrespective of diverse social and cultural contexts, and of community custodians of life enhancing systems and traditions.
- To build bridges among diverse language communities, and thereby to strengthen the foundations of a multilingual, multicultural Indian society.
- To create closer links between the government and speech communities, and to bring the universal developmental strategies of the government in harmony with ecologically and culturally diverse communities.
- To develop teaching material and capability for promoting education in the mother tongue.
- To provide a baseline for any future survey of India's linguistic and cultural composition.
- To arrest the extinction of linguistic, cultural and biological diversity, nurtured by speech communities over generations, and to protect one of the few surviving bastions of linguistic diversity in the world in the interest of human security and survival.

The National Editorial Collective

Madhya Pradesh
Damodar Jain

Maharashtra
Arun Jakhade

Manipur
K. Nipuni Mao
Kownigly Wangla

Meghalaya
Esther Syiem

Mizoram
Cherrie Lalnunziri Chhangte
L. Thangi Chhangte

Nagaland
D. Koulie

Odisha
D. P. Pattanayak
M. K. Mishra

Punjab
Omkar N. Koul
Roop Kishen Bhat

Rajasthan
Madan Meena
Surajmal Rao

Sikkim
Balaram Pandey

Tamil Nadu
V. Gnansundaram
K. Rangan

Tripura
Sukhendu Debbarma

Uttar Pradesh
Ashish Kumar Anshu
Badri Narayan

Uttarakhand
Shekhar Pathak
Uma Bhatt

West Bengal
Sankar Singha
Indranil Acharya

UNION TERRITORIES

Andaman and Nicobar Islands
Francis Neelam

Dadra & Nagar Haveli
Kanji Patel

Daman and Diu
Kanji Patel

Lakshadweep
M. Sreenathan

Puducherry
L. Ramamoorthy
G. Ravisankar

PAN-INDIAN LANGUAGES

Avadhesh K. Singh
L. Khubchandani
Sukrita Paul Kumar
T. Vijay Kumar
B. Mallikarjun

Translation Advisors

Avadhesh K. Singh
Ipshita Chanda
Tutun Mukherjee
Nila Shah

Sign Languages

Nisha Grover
Tanmoy Bhattacharya
Surinder P. K. Randhawa

List of Volumes

Volume 1

The Being of Bhasha: A General Introduction

G. N. Devy

Part One—Hindi

Part Two—English

Volume 2

The Languages of Andaman and Nicobar Islands

Edited by M. Sreenathan

Part One—Hindi

Part Two—English

Volume 3

The Languages of Andhra Pradesh and Telangana

Edited by A.Usha Devi and Chandra Sekhar Reddy

Part One—Hindi

Part Two—English

Part Three—Telugu

Volume 4

The Languages of Arunachal Pradesh

Edited by Lisa Lomdak

Part One—Hindi

Part Two—English

Volume 5

The Languages of Assam

Edited by Bibha Bharali and Banani Chakravarty

Part One—Hindi

Part Two—English

Part Three—Assamese

Volume 6

The Languages of Bihar

Edited by Vibha Chauhan

Part One—Hindi

Part Two—English

Volume 7

The Languages of Chhattisgarh

Edited by Chitta Ranjan Kar

Part One—Hindi

Part Two—English

Volume 8

The Languages of Goa

Edited by Madhavi Sardesai

Part One—Hindi

Part Two—English

Volume 9

The Languages of Gujarat, Diu & Daman and Dadra & Nagar Haveli
Edited by Kanji Patel
Part One—Hindi
Part Two—English
Part Three—Gujarati

Volume 10

The Languages of Haryana
Edited by Roop Krishen Bhat and Omkar N. Koul
Part One—Hindi
Part Two—English

Volume 11

The Languages of Himachal Pradesh
Edited by Tobdan
Part One—Hindi
Part Two—English

Volume 12

The Languages of Jammu & Kashmir
Edited by Omkar N. Koul
Part One—Hindi
Part Two—English

Volume 13

The Languages of Jharkhand
Edited by Ramnika Gupta and Prabhatkumar Singh
Part One—Hindi
Part Two—English

Volume 14

The Languages of Karnataka
Edited by Rajeshwari Maheshwariah and M. Maheshwariah
Part One—Hindi
Part Two—English
Part Three—Kannada

Volume 15

The Languages of Kerala and Lakshadweep
Edited by M. Sreenathan and Joseph Koyippally
Part One—Hindi
Part Two—English

Volume 16

The Languages of Madhya Pradesh
Part One—Hindi
Edited by Damodar Singh Jain
Part Two—English
Edited by Prashant Mishra

Volume 17

The Languages of Maharashtra
Edited by Arun Jakhade
Part One—Marathi
Part Two—English
Part Three—Marathi

Volume 18

The Languages of Manipur
Edited by Nipuni Mao
Part One—Hindi
Part Two—English

Volume 19

The Languages of Meghalaya
Edited by Esther Syiem
Part One—Hindi
Part Two—English
Part Three—Khashi and Garo

Volume 20

The Languages of Mizoram
Edited by L. Thangi Chhangte
Part One—Hindi
Part Two—English

Volume 21

The Languages of Nagaland
Edited by Duovituo Kuolie
Part One—Hindi
Part Two—English

Volume 22

The Languages of Odisha
Edited by D. P. Pattanayak
and Mahendra Kumar Mishra
Part One—Hindi
Part Two—English
Part Three—Odiya

Volume 23

The Languages of Puducherry
Edited by L Ramamoorthy and G. Ravisankar
Part One—Hindi
Part Two—English

Volume 24

The Languages of Punjab
Edited by Omkar N. Koul and Roop Krishen Bhat
Part One—Hindi
Part Two—English

Volume 25

The Languages of Rajasthan
Edited by Madan Meena and Suraj Mal Rao
Part One—Hindi
Part Two—English

Volume 26

The Languages of Sikkim
Edited by Balaram Pandey
Part One—Hindi
Part Two—English
Part Three—Nepali

Volume 27

The Languages of Tamil Nadu
Edited by V. Gnanasundaram and K. Rangan
Part One—Hindi
Part Two—English
Part Three—Tamil

Volume 28

The Languages of Tripura
Edited by Sukhendu Debbarma
Part One—Hindi
Part Two—English

Volume 29

The Languages of Uttar Pradesh
Edited by Badri Narayan
Part One—Hindi
Part Two—English

Volume 30

The Languages of Uttarakhand
Edited by Uma Bhatt and Shekhar Pathak
Part One—Hindi
Part Two—English

Volume 31

The Languages of West Bengal
Edited by Sankar Singha and Indranil Acharya
Part One—Hindi
Part Two—English
Part Three—Bangla

Volume 32

The Scheduled Languages—Assamiya,
Bangla, Bodo, Maithili,
Manipuri, Oriya, Nepali and Santali
Edited by G. N. Devy and Nipuni Mao

Volume 33

The Scheduled Languages—Dogri, Kashmiri,
Punjabi and Urdu
Edited by Omkar N. Koul

Volume 34

The Scheduled Languages—Gujarati, Konkani,
Marathi, Sindhi
Edited by G. N. Devy

Volume 35

The Scheduled Languages—Kannada, Malayalam, Tamil and Telugu
Edited by V. Gnanasundaram and K. Rangan

Volume 36

The Scheduled Languages—Sanskrit and Hindi
Edited by Avadhesh K. Singh

Volume 37

English and Other International Languages
Part One—*European—English, French and Portuguese*
Edited by T. Vijay Kumar
Part Two—*Asian—Arabic, Karen, Nepali, Persian, Syriac and Tibetan*
Edited by Sukrita Paul Kumar

Volume 38

Indian Sign Language(s)
Edited by Tanmoy Bhattacharya, Nisha Grover and Surinder P. K. Randhawa
Part One—Hindi
Part Two—English

Volume 39

Shared Languages of the Indian Subcontinent
Edited by Sukrita Paul Kumar

Volume 40

The Tribal Languages—The North-Eastern States
Edited by G. N. Devy

Volume 41

The Tribal Languages—The Eastern States—Bengal, Bihar, Jharkhand and Orissa
Edited by G. N. Devy

Volume 42

The Tribal Languages—Central Indian States—Chhattisgarh, Gujarat, Madhya Pradesh, Maharashtra and Rajasthan
Edited by G. N. Devy

Volume 43

The Tribal Languages—The Southern States and the Islands
Edited by G. N. Devy

Volume 44

The Tribal Languages of the North-West and the Himalayan States
Edited by Omkar N. Koul

Volume 45

Language Census, Survey and Policy
Edited by B. Mallikarjun

Volume 46

Scripts in India
Edited by G. N. Devy

Volume 47

Indian Languages in the Diaspora
Edited by T. Vijay Kumar

Volume 48

Comparative Wordlist—Kinship and Social Relations
Edited by G. N. Devy

Volume 49

Comparative Wordlist—Time and Space
Edited by G. N. Devy

Volume 50

The Future of Indian Languages
Edited by G. N. Devy
Part One—Hindi
Part Two—English

Acknowledgements

It is our pride to mention the consistent support, patient guidance and impeccable advice from Professor Ganesh Devy, the Chief Editor of this volume and who is also the Chairperson of the People's Linguistic Survey of India. We thank him wholeheartedly for standing with us throughout the preparation of this volume.

The content of this volume is the outcome of the research carried out by the editors. As editors of this volume we are very grateful to all those whose work helped us in completing this work.

Foreword

While thinking about the *People's Linguistic Survey of India*, it suddenly struck me that the Indian Constitution opens with the words, 'We the people of India'. In the context of the debate about the supremacy of the Parliament and the Supreme Court, we have forgotten the people of India. Although people have the supremacy, they are not contestants of Parliament or the Supreme Court. Similarly, PLSI is neither a contestant of Grierson's survey or the survey conducted by the Registrar General of India. It is an independent, autonomous, people oriented and people motivated survey, trying to capture the perception of the people about the languages they speak. The PLSI aims at restoring the self confidence of the people that their languages are good for education, administration and mass communication. They are good for development and for intimate communication. Once their self confidence is restored, they will know that the mother tongue is the best foundation for learning more languages and subjects. Mother tongue helps in sharing as well as caring.

Indian intellectuals have contributed a word, 'mainstreaming', to the English dictionary. Mainstreaming is excluding, marginalising and demolishing smaller languages and cultures. It is another name for genocide. The tribals in particular, who are displaced from their habitat in the forests and mountains, are wrenched from their languages and cultures are forced to adopt the dominant regional language as their mother tongue. Hindi is considered the mainstream for many Indian languages and English is the mainstream for all Indian languages including Hindi. All binaries such as primitive-civilised, simple-advanced, low-high, concrete-abstract, pre-logical-analytical, utterance-text, are manipulated to defend dominance and subjugation. They are 'socialisation into mainstream ways of using language in speech and print, mainstream ways of making meaning, of making sense of experience.'* From the mainstream point of view orality is an evil which needs determined eradication. Indian society is a relation based society, clearly different from the binary and contract based society of the West. This is what explains the extended family, the extended society and the language and culture area. Thousands of years ago it was said,

ayam nija parobetti gaNana laghu cetasam.
udara caritanantu basudheiba kutumbakam

---

* Gee, James Paul. 1994. Oracy and Literacy: From *The savage mind* to *ways with words*. In *Language and Literacy in Social Practice: A Reader*, ed. J. Maybin, 168–92. The Open Univerisity: Multilingual Matters.

> The self and the other distinction is made by the narrow/light minded ones. The broad minded ones bind the whole universe in a network of relations.

At the societal level it is seen in the intensity of retailers in India. India is the most intense retailer based society in the world, with one retailer for eight Indians. This is the best realisation of relation based society at the socio-economic level. Language, religion, caste and community, unity in variation, is another example. India, with 3000 mother tongues, 4000 castes and communities, 4000 faiths and beliefs presents a variation not found anywhere in the world. And yet bound by a network of relations, their unity of relation is incomparable. In spite of languages belonging to six language families, India is recognised, by scholars of the world as a single language, linguistic and semantic area. Ever since pundits named languages and designated some as languages and others as dialects, hierarchical organisation of languages began to take shape. It was forgotten that each language is a dialect. There is no language without a dialect and no dialect without a language. Pundits' languages were distanced from the peoples' perception of languages. Pundits' languages are dominant, monolingual and exclusive. Peoples' languages are multiple, variant repertoires with language complementation. They are inclusive with ideolect to universal language, bound by a single thread. By refusing the people to recognise the right to name we deny their existence and once they die we museumise them. All surveys are for selection. Failure to share is failure to care. Extinction of language is not merely extinction of orality, it is extinction of bio-cultural knowledge. PLSI reinforced the conclusion that to look for a monolingual in a multilingual setting is a fiction. In the developed countries of the West, bilingualism was considered an extension of monolingualism, and multilingualism an aberration. Bilingualism at one time was considered negative subtractive and a burden, and multilingualism as no language. It was forgotten that monolingualism and bilingualism has an isolating, 'either/or' role whereas multilingualism has an inclusive identity, 'both/and' role. Here an individual or community has multiple identities and roles.

The PLSI gives important clues about language acquisition and language instruction. A multilingual child does not learn one language after another and one skill after another. A multilingual child learns many languages together. A language acquired without formal tuition till the age of four is the mother tongue of the child. A language taught in the classroom, where the language is spoken in the immediate environment is a second language. A language confined to the classroom is a foreign language. The implication of such understanding is that a child has more than one mother tongue, more than one second language and an Indian language may be taught as a foreign language within the country. Learning is neither hierarchical nor linear. In a rural society where people learn many languages from the environment without schooling, where they require literacy for communicating with the world beyond their immediate environment, as well as in the case of the international, formally educated, multilingual post modern elite nomad who disclaim specific mother tongues, where languages and literacy are required for socio-economic mobility within the country (nationally) or outside (internationally) and where mother tongue itself is multilingual, the first language-second language distinction in serial order is meaningless.

In language learning as opposed to language acquisition the monolingual hierarchy still persists. Whether it is first language, second language or foreign language, or the four skills of listening, speaking, reading, writing, these are hierarchically organised. Bereft of pedagogical implications, the same language is taught as first, second or third language depending on the order of introduction in the school.

It is evident that there is no meaningful research about multilingualism in general and the multilingual child in particular. If the findings of the PLSI create awareness and acceptance of multilingualism as the foundation of education and this results in serious research, then the project will be justified. If it helps in building bridges between academic language and culture on the one hand and popular, cultural and developmental on the other, then the project will have been successful.

D. P. Pattanayak
Convener, National Editorial Collective
People's Linguistic Survey of India

A Nation Proud of Its Language Diversity

Chief Editor's Introduction

The Global Language Crisis

Over the last two decades, scientists have come up with mathematical models for predicting the life of languages. These predictions have invariably indicated that the human species is moving rapidly close to extinction of a large part of its linguistic heritage. These predictions do not agree on the exact magnitude of the impending disaster; but they all agree on the fact that close to three quarters or over of all existing natural human languages are half in the grave. There are, on the other hand, advocates of linguistic globalisation. They would prefer the spread of one or only a few languages all over the world so that communication across national boundaries becomes the easiest ever. Obviously, the nations and communities that have learnt to live within only a single language, whose economic well being is not dependent on knowing languages other than their own, whose knowledge systems are well secured within their own languages, will not experience the stress of language loss, at least not immediately, though the loss of the world's total language heritage, which will weaken the global stock of human intellect and civilisations, will have numerous indirect enfeebling effects on them too. Since it is language mainly, of all things, that makes us human and distinguishes us from other species and animate nature, and since the human consciousness can but function given the ability for linguistic expression, it becomes necessary to recognise language as the most crucial aspect of cultural capital. It has taken us continuous work of about half a million years to accumulate this valuable capital. In our time we have come close to the point of losing most of it. Some of the predictions maintain that out of an approximately 6000 existing languages, not more than 300 will survive in the twenty-second century. In absence of thorough surveys of languages, it is difficult to decide as to how many languages really are in existence; and it is even more difficult to predict how many of these, and precisely which ones, will survive. History of every language has strange and sometimes completely unpredictable outcomes. The recent upward trend of some of the tribal languages in India such as Bhilli can be an example. It defies all established sociolinguistic assumptions. In history, some mighty languages, supported by mighty empires are seen to disintegrate and give rise to new languages under the influence of the ones on the power margins. But, while these amazing exceptions do exist, and will continue to emerge in future as well, it is a lived experience of people in countries like Nigeria, Mexico, Papua New Guinea, Indonesia and India that most languages are passing through the phase of a rapid depletion in domains of language transaction and word stocks. The ability of speakers of non-global languages to express complex concepts is seen to being alarmingly reduced; and the semantic layering of words in most languages is wearing off.

Historians of civilisation tell us that probably a comparable, though obviously not exactly similar, situation had arisen in the past, some seven or eight thousand years ago. This was when human beings discovered the magic of nature that seeds are. When the shift from an entirely hunting, gathering or pastoralist, economies to early agrarian economies started taking place, we are told, the language diversity of the world got severely affected. It may not be wrong to surmise that the current crisis in human languages too is triggered by the fundamental economic shift that has enveloped the entire world, north or south, west or east. This time, though, the crisis has an added theme as a lot of the human activity is dominated by artificial intelligence. The technologies aligned with artificial intelligence have all been depending heavily on modelling the activity of the human mind along linguistic transactions. The intelligent machines modelled after neurological and psychological paths of the mind are still not commonly in use. Language-based technologies are now well entrenched partners in the semantic universes that bind human communities together. Therefore, those universes (or that universe?) are being re-shaped and re-constructed. In the given situation, though all this can be conceptualised in philosophic terms or presented in sociological formula, it is the life of the communities that is getting affected. It is particularly the communities whose voices do not get heard that are at the receiving end in the phenomenal transition. Having a language of your own, not yet placed within any system of orthographic representation, has come to be seen as a liability, a developmental debacle and a sign of backwardness. The knowledge stock in these languages is being trashed as non-knowledge. The countries mentioned above, which have a large number of languages developed over centuries—Papua New Guinea, 900; India, 700; Indonesia, 600; Nigeria, 400; Mexico, 300—assessed through varying kind of estimates, have started forgetting that the rich variety is their cultural capital. In our country, census authorities decided after the 1971 census exercise that there was no need to disclose the statistics for languages spoken by less than 10,000 persons, in turn making those languages 'non-citizens' of the republic of languages that India has been all through its history. The census decision during the 1970s was, of course, not an abrupt or sudden decision. The process was initiated during colonial times, the period when about two per cent of India's languages were committed to print. Besides, it was a culmination of the intellectual history that was in the making over the last two centuries.

I first read George A. Grierson's *Linguistic Survey of India* during the 1970s. As a young reader of his monumental work what struck me most was not the amazing range of his knowledge of India's language situation, nor his determination to complete the task in the face of enormous challenges. These, it is needless to say, will leave no reader unaffected. The most overwhelming feature of Grierson's survey that I noticed was the silent spaces in them. Even at the beginning of the twentieth century, which was Grierson's time, one notices through his account the beginning of a slow death spelt for nearly a hundred and sixty-five out of the hundred and seventy-nine languages that he had documented and described. I am not aware of any full scale comparison between Grierson's 'linguistic discovery of India' with a similar discovery by his eminent predecessor Sir William Jones. Jones was excited about the presence of 'different' languages in India, though of course he had no way to know how many of them existed in his time. In contrast, Grierson's description had no such 'eureka' about it. When one reads the Grierson volumes, one returns home with the impression that these are in most part rustic varieties, fit only for housing childish songs and materials good enough for folklorists subservient to Anthropology. As against the less than two hundred languages that he described, he had over five hundred dialects to describe. The arithmetic of the great work is indicative of its essential bias. Perhaps, the beginning of it was embedded in William Jones's work, despite his apparent euphoria in discovering India as an unknown continent of civilisation.

The Silenced Oral

Since the times of Sir William Jones, major attempts have been made to propose and formulate cognitive categories for describing the bio-cultural diversity and knowledge traditions in India. The corresponding process of de-colonisation too has produced attempts at synchronisation of traditional knowledge with the colonial production of knowledge within the context of western modernity. While the clash as well as collaboration between what is seen as knowledge compatible with western cognitive categories and knowledge traditions rooted in the lives of predominantly oral communities continue to occupy the imaginative transactions in India, the mainstream institutions of knowledge—such as schools, universities, hospitals, courts, etc.—have acquired forms that often leave out the complexities involved in the 'great transition of civilisation in the Indian sub-continent.' This situation poses an intellectual challenge that thinkers in the twenty-first century have to negotiate. The most important among the cognitive categories that continue to carry the stress of this 'transition in civilisation' belong to the field of creative expression in language and language description. Decolonisation of Indian aesthetics and Indian linguistics, without an obscurantist turning back entirely to the past, is the larger task at hand for the contemporary Indian intellectual. In recent times there have been moves towards opening the question of descriptive categories in relation to language and orality. This has been the most central focus of the *People's Linguistic Survey of India* (PLSI). Describing languages is the method that the PLSI has adopted for serving the purpose. Therefore, the PLSI has consciously decided to stay away from the question that historical linguistics follows, namely the question of the origin and the family of a given language. The PLSI has adopted, instead, an apparently ahistorical method of presenting merely a snap-shot of languages as they are in the early years of the twenty-first century. Apart from the principle of determining language identity in terms of its filial relation with a given language family, the most ardently followed principle from Jones to Grierson, and a lot beyond them, was that of the language and dialect distinction. I decided after thinking through nearly three decades and after numerous prolonged discussions with my colleagues in communities and within the PLSI Editorial Collective to avoid branding any of the languages as dialects. If a large number of people who speak a given language think that it is a language and not a dialect, then it is better that it is accepted as a language, even if linguistics may find the claim untenable. In any case, linguistics, while it has made very impressive progress through the last two centuries as a field of study, has still a long way to go before it can address all and every mystery surrounding the behaviour of verbal signs used by human beings for externalising the complex and abstract transactions. The question of dialects too is one of those yet unsettled.

Language and Reality

The process of human evolution holds many secrets. Our inadequate understanding of the process leads us to build apparently scientific hypotheses. But these hypotheses are such that even the exactly contrary hypotheses sound equally convincing. Language as a social institution, the nature of its exact origin, and the clear sequence in its formation are some of the mysteries in the epic text of human evolution.

Was there an attendant sound when the universe came into existence? Did sound exist at all prior to the animal ability to perceive sound? Do the eternal sound—the *anahat dhvani*—and the sound by vocal cords belong to the same material type? Why did the human animal select regulation of breath by the vocal cords as the means for transacting meaning, while the same transaction through the eyes or through body movement (as with bees) might have been equally effective? Why did the human animal not pursue those other means of expression with equal emphasis? All these questions can be answered at a theoretical level; but the answers do not cross the level of philosophical propositions that are true but at the same time not entirely so.

Regulation of air by the vocal cords came to be the central mode of transacting meaning at some stage in the evolution of the intellect, subsequently numerical and letters—a higher order of signs—became surrogates for sound. Why did not then the script language entirely displace the sound language?

While the theory of language acquisition inherent in the psychic structure of an infant has been formulated, why is that no theory as yet been postulated regarding the natural ability to perceive the *correspondence between* those geometrical shapes called letters and the human sounds called syllables?

'Meaning' consists of the meaning expressed through gesticulations, sound regulation and script marks as well as through the silence and stillness outside the pale of these three. Therefore, what exactly constitutes 'meaning' has not been conclusively determined. At the most, the theories of meaning have remained at the level of philosophical speculation. Besides, it has not been possible so far to state with precision as to whether meaning is language, or if meaning existed before languages came into being, and if it is yet another social or metaphysical system completely independent of verbal language, capable of transcending human language. It is true that language as an experiential phenomenon is within the range of an individual's perception, but it is also true that an individual's ability to perceive the world is conditioned by verbal language. This has led us to conclude that language is a social institution.

But is language 'meaning', or is it some material 'thing'? Is it a transcendental energy or a purely social institution? Is it a mere biological function given to the human body and mind in the process of evolution? Or is it all of these at once or in various aspects of the language phenomenon? All these questions need to be tackled fully despite linguistics being the most developed among the human sciences.

There is a well-established view that culture has no other expression but language, that the two are one and the same. It is maintained that cognition too would be impossible without language. A similar view on meaning too exists. In other words, 'language' has been used as a synonym for that which determines the outer boundaries of each transaction of the human intelligence.

Even when the structure of dreams is not based on language content, it is conceptualised as being the same as language structure; the origin of dreams is in the ability to remember, in memory. In other words we are made to believe that memory cannot exist entirely in absence of language. Similarly, we have come to believe that other psychic possibilities such as inspiration, imagination and reason cannot exist in the absence of language.

While these hypotheses seem unexceptionable, it is true that there are experiences that the human animal shares with other animals that show a marked absence of language based on sound regulation. Vertigo, or the fear of falling, and love or sensuous attraction are the main instances of such experiences.

Phenomenology, which is one of the sciences of human understanding, maintains that language develops 'in tune' with the perpetually increasing scope of the phenomenon perceived by the human mind. As against this, it has been argued that the human grasp of this phenomenal reality increases in proportion to the ever-increasing ability of language to grasp complexities. It is indeed difficult to establish if a domain of experience exists independently and outside the domain of language. At the same time it is even more difficult to overrule the existence of such a domain of experience.

It is similarly a complicated question as to whether those semi-verbal or verbal components that scripts, grammars and cultures, but are not considered 'language' are languages or not? At best they find a place in marginal categories such as dialects and regional varieties.

In fact, in the vast spectrum of meaning beginning with the mysterious origin of sound, to its pervasive spread through human space and time, human languages may at best be seen as dialects of the uninterrupted *dhvani.*

Similarly, in the total range of meaning capable of being conducted through material and symbolic means, the sound-symbol based language will have to be counted as a dialect of the total range of meaning.

Moreover, the process of the perpetual enlargement and deepening of our understanding of the world indicates the possibility that, perhaps, the language-substance known to us at the present stage of our evolution is but a partial fraction of the ultimate possibilities of the meaning substance available to the human senses. Therefore, in some ways language will have to be thought of as a part, as a dialect, of the totality of experience. And the totality of the human languages stabilised through words and scripts will have to be seen as a dialect of the totality of all experience, all meaning and all sound as a single entity. Therefore, a dialect does not mean being left behind but means being *avant-garde*.

One can understand the true nature of dialect if one conceptualises it as a necessary component, not as a decaying remnant, of language. The destiny of dialects is to be at the turbulent interface of an ever expanding reality, to be the 'advance party' for grasping untapped frontiers of meaning. Histories of languages show that it has been their fate to keep catching up with the dialects, not the other way round. The destiny of dialects is to persist in their exploration of new possibilities of meaning, albeit without losing their relationship with the standardised languages to which they are bound by political and historical circumstances. The destiny of a dialect is to remain in currency but, unfortunately, with the value of the counterfeit.

To use a metaphor, dialect is like the amorphous substance surrounding a newly born planet, which is yet to find its ultimate rate of revolution. The planet environment of the language is defined by its dialects. It is through them that languages keep their ceaseless contact with the universe outside them, and therefore manage to belong to it.

So far it has been maintained that the speech variety of the dominant class acquires the status of the standard language, whereas the speech varieties of the dominated are seen as dialects. This view is based on the history of the English language in England. But going by this logic the Hindi spoken by politically dominant Indians should have by now become the standard variety of Hindi, and the Marathi of the Maratha rulers should have become its main variety. This however has not been so. The Indian experience indicates that the history of English in England does not provide enough scientific foundation for a universal dialectology.

Besides, for cultures where the politically dominant class often speaks a non-native language, and where the culturally dominant class has not been monolingual, dialects have to be thought about all over again.

If we set aside this unanswered equation and postulate that language is a means of bringing the ever expanding universe of experience within the grasp of human understanding, then it follows that dialects (or sub-languages) have a place of primary importance in the process of internalisation of meaning for a given language.

In this process, it becomes necessary to achieve a meaningful amalgamation of new sensations with the most ancient memories. While achieving this amalgamation, dialects put to stake their existence and identity, and bring to a given language an enriched sensitivity and ability to express.

A language without dialects will tend to become a meaningless bundle of clichés. In such a situation words will become meaningless abstractions. Perhaps such a language might achieve out of its grammatical purity the power of perfect mathematical abstraction. But its sound tokens will be so impersonal that they will altogether alienate the 'animal' user, with a living consciousness.

A language must have personality. Human beings will carry the burden of language as long as they feel proud of belonging to their respective languages.

For centuries, European linguists have made attempts at tracing the one original language, the mother of all languages. Behind these attempts was probably the myth of the Tower of Babel, where the one, the original language, was confounded into innumerable others. Consequently, dialects have come to be viewed as the backyard of language. These backyards are really the sources of their being and growth. The dialects, sub-languages, language varieties and the backyard tongues are the energy that has kept the stream of Indian languages flowing. To continue the metaphor of the stream, the so-called main languages are its banks; the dialects are the flow of the stream. To keep the streams going is the least that we should do.

Marginal Voices

In the pre-colonial epistemologies of language, hierarchy in terms of a 'standard' and a 'dialect' was not common. Language diversity was an accepted fact of life. Literary artists could use several languages within a single composition, and their audience accepted the practice as normal. Great works like the *Mahabharata* continued to exist in several versions handed down through a number of different languages almost till the beginning of the twentieth century. When literary critics theorised, they took into account literature in numerous languages. Matanga's medieval compendium of styles, *Brihad-deshi*, is an outstanding example of criticism arising out of the principle that language diversity is normal. During colonial times, many Indian languages were brought into the realm of printing. Earlier too, writing was known and numerous scripts were already in use. Paper too was used as a means for reproducing written texts. However, despite being 'written', texts had been in circulation mostly orally. Printing technology gradually diminished the existing oral traditions. New norms of literature were introduced, privileging the written over the oral, and propagating the idea that a literary text needs be essentially monolingual. These ideas, and the power relation prevailing in the colonial context, started affecting the stock of languages in India. The languages that did not have any printed material came to be seen as 'inferior' languages. After independence, the Indian states were created on the basis of languages and are known as 'linguistic states'. If a language had a script, and if the language had *printed* literature in it, it was given a geographical zone as a separate state within the Union of India. Languages that did not have printed literature, even though they had a rich tradition of oral literature, were not given such states. Further, the state official language was used as a medium of primary and high-school education within a given state. Similarly, a special 'Schedule of Languages' (The Eighth Schedule) was created within the Indian Constitution. In the beginning it had a list of fourteen languages. At present the list has twenty-two languages It became obligatory for the government to commit all education related expenditure on these languages alone. The 1961 census of India had a list of 1652 'mother tongues'. In the findings of the next census (1971), the figure was substantially reduced, and only 108 languages spoken by more than 10,000 were officially acknowledged. Thus, nearly 1500 'mother tongues' were silenced. Most of these languages are spoken by nomadic communities and the indigenous communities. Most of these languages are on way to a rapid extinction, if they are not already extinct. The 'margins' of the Indian language spectrum, constituted by indigenous peoples and the nomadic communities are thus marginalised mainly due to the 'aphasia' being systemically imposed on them. The PLSI is a collective effort by the people of India to register their 'voices'. It is not a repeat, or a replacement or a substitute for Grierson's surveys. The parameters for the accomplishments of those surveys are different. The PLSI is more of an informal attempt to bring to the world's notice the phenomenal language diversity in India, and by extension in the rest of the world, in the interest of keeping the biosphere alive, and preserving the democracy that India has acquired through a long and arduous struggle.

It is a daunting task to determine as to which languages have come closest to the condition of aphasia, which ones are decidedly moving in that direction and which ones are merely going through the natural linguistic process of transmigration. It may not be inappropriate to say that the linguistic data available with us is not enough to make an accurate assessment.

In India, Grierson's *Linguistic Survey of India* (1903–1923)—material for which was collected in the last decade of the 19th century—had identified 179 languages and 544 dialects. The 1921 census reports showed 188 languages and 49 dialects.

In 1971, the linguistic data offered in the census was distributed in two categories, the officially listed languages of the Eighth Schedule of the Constitution, and the other languages with a minimum of 10,000 speakers each. All other languages spoken by less than 10,000 speakers were put together in a single entry, 'Others'.

Considering how complicated the census operations are in countries that have large migratory populations, and particularly how much the accuracy in census operations is dependent on literacy levels, it is not surprising that the data collected remains insufficiently definitive. What is surprising, however, is that as many as 310 languages, including all those 263 claimed by less than five speakers, and 47 others claimed by less than a 1000 speakers, should have reached endangerment. These 310 'endangered' languages are among the 1652 'mother tongues' listed in the census of 1961, however debatable the methodology followed in that particular census may have been. In other words, a fifth part of India's linguistic heritage has reached the stage of extinction over the last half-century. Moreover, the method of survey adopted over the last three census enumerations allows scope for overlooking any further depletion in the numbers.

One fears that this may not be the situation in only one country, but that this might perhaps be so throughout the world, since the contextual factors responsible for language decline in one country also form the context of modernity in other nation states in the world.

Language loss is experienced in India not just by the 'minor' languages and 'unclassified dialects', but also by 'major' languages that have long literary traditions and a rich heritage of imaginative and philosophical writings. In speech communities that claim major literary languages such as Marathi, Gujarati, Kannada and Odiya as their 'mother tongues', the younger generations have little or no contact with the written heritage of those languages, though they are able to speak the languages as native speakers. This linguistic condition may be described as the condition of 'partial language acquisition' in which a fully literate person, with a relatively high degree of education, is able to read, write and speak a language other than her/his mother tongue, but is able to only speak but not write the language she/he claims as her/his mother tongue.

Language loss, linguistic shifts and decline in the linguistic heritage cannot be blamed on the structural factors alone. There is, for instance, at least as a theoretical constitutional provision, the Article 347, which reads:

> On a demand made in that behalf, the President may, if he is satisfied that a substantial proportion of the population of the State desire the use of any language spoken by them to be recognized by that State, direct that such language shall also be officially recognized throughout that State, or any part thereof, for such purposes as he may specify.

Another more overwhelming factor seems to be at work in a rapidly globalising world, and that is the prevailing discourse of economic development. One now notices in India, and in other Asian and African countries, the overpowering desire among parents to educate their children through the medium of English or French or Spanish, in the hope that these languages will provide their children a linguistic advantage in the international market of productive labour. This has affected the schooling pattern in favour of education through an international language not seen in any previous era.

During the early years of the nineteenth century, an interesting debate occupied the centre-stage in the social reform movement in India, in which the Bengali intellectuals kept asking for education through the English language medium, while an English officer like Mountstuart Elphinstone held that the schools in Indian languages would be desirable. The argument came to an end when in 1835, Lord Macaulay's *Minutes on Education* held that English be the medium of all serious education in India, a view endorsed soon after in Wood's *Dispatch*. Quite remarkably, it was since then that literatures in modern Indian languages showed a significant creativity. These arguments are not intended to take away any substance from the view that mother tongue education is the most suitable for young learners. I am only pointing to the fact that a lack of access to mother tongue education by itself is not enough to destroy human creativity. The destruction is greater if the community loses the hope of its very survival altogether.

When a speech community comes to believe that education in some other language alone is the way ahead for it for its very survival, the community decides to adapt to the new language situation. It would be worthwhile therefore to consider if there is something inherent in the dominant development discourse in the contemporary world that leads to the diminishing of world's language heritage, or demands a kind of a *phonocide*. And, if that is the case, the future of human languages is frightening. The communities that are already marginalised within their local or national context, the ones that are already in minority within their cultural contexts, the ones that have already been dispossessed of their ability to voice their concerns, are obviously placed at the frontline of the *phonocide*.

In India, universal education is the obligation of parents and the right of the child. State sponsored schooling is almost free and clearly affordable even for the most deprived. There is provision of mid-day meals for children so that food insecurity does not drive children away from classrooms. The federal government and the state governments treat school education as one of their primary responsibilities. Child labour is officially made illegal, and even higher education is made free for women in many states. There are provisions for educational reservations for children belonging to schedule castes and scheduled tribes as also for children from other backward communities. The Indian State operates primary schools in nearly fifty Indian languages and several foreign languages. Adult literacy and non-formal schooling are continuously promoted. There are constitutional guarantees built in the educational programmes aimed at promoting all listed languages.

In spite of such efforts, many marginalised languages and indeed some of the 'major' languages seem to display an inscrutable indifference towards their upkeep. An unimaginably large number of children seem to join schools that charge exorbitant fees and have English as the medium of instruction. When a child joins a school where the medium of instruction is an Indian language, it is seen as the beginning of a social disadvantage. Under these circumstances, the preservation of languages, particularly the ones that need really very special efforts aimed at their preservation, is quite a daunting task and not one that can be accomplished merely by initiating structural changes

Conservation or preservation of languages needs to be seen as being significantly different from the preservation of monuments. Though language as a social system has an objective existence in the sense that dictionaries and grammars of languages can be prepared, and languages can be transcribed, orthographed, mimeographed, recorded on a tape by way of documents and objects, yet language does not have an existence entirely free of the human consciousness. Therefore, a given language cannot be as completely dissociated from the community that uses it. Quite logically, therefore, preservation of a language entails the preservation of the community that puts that language in circulation.

Between the collective consciousness of a given community, and the language it uses to articulate the consciousness, is situated what is described as the 'world view' of that community. Preservation of a language involves, therefore, respecting the world view of that speech community. If such a community believes that the human destiny is to belong to the earth and not to offend the earth by claiming that it belongs to us, the language of that community cannot be preserved when we invite the community to share a political imagination that believes in vandalising the earth's resources in the name of development. In such a situation, the community will have only two options: it can either reject the *utopia* that asserts the human right to exploit the natural resources and turn them into exclusively commercial commodities, or it can reject its own world view and step out of the language system that binds it with the world view.

Indeed, the situation of the languages in the world, more particularly the languages of the indigenous peoples, marginalised and minority communities and of the cultures that have experienced or continue to experience alien cultural domination, has become precarious. The alarm to be raised will not be even a day too soon. Yet, it would be ambitious to hope that this task can be achieved even in a small degree by merely placing the onus and the responsibility solely on state parties. The mission will have to be carried out, through the agency of the nation states, and independent of it, through a large number of civil society actors—universities, literary and linguistic academies, goodwill societies and associations, non-governmental organisations, individual scholars, researchers and activists. Creation of texts, dictionaries, glossaries and grammars in the declining languages will be of use; documentation, museumisation and archiving too will be of some use; but if the languages are expected to survive, the speech communities need to be given the dignity and respect that they deserve, not as anthropological others, not as the last and underdeveloped traces of the self, but in their own right as deserving of respect because of what they are.

It takes centuries for a community to create a language. All languages created by human communities are our collective cultural heritage. Therefore, it is our collective responsibility to ensure that they do not face the global phonocide let loose in our time.

The *People's Linguistic Survey of India* conceptualised during the early years of Bhasha Research Centre, an idea that found a clear articulation in the *Bhasha Sangam*, 2010, held at Baroda under the name *Language Confluence at Ground* Zero. It had at its heart the concerns stated in my comments. I was fortunate to be asked by the large assembly, in which representatives of 320 Indian languages were present, to lead the PLSI. The first workshop in that direction was held at Kyelang in Himachal Pradesh, in freezing cold when the rest of India suffered the summer heat. I am not able to say how many such workshops were held since then, for rarely do I remember a day when I have not been in the middle of the survey. This required travelling through all the states and union territories of India. Though, in the past, I had travelled to many states for other work, and to many other countries, the PLSI sojourn brought to me an India that I had never before seen and had only vaguely imagined. People responded enthusiastically to our call, asking them to write about their languages. These included vice-chancellors of universities as well as bus drivers, scholars and street singers, law keepers as well as criminals, men and women, the young and the old. They sat together, listened to me, spent their time and wrote down what they knew about their languages. Most of them do not know what grammar is. They are not aware of the International Phonetic Apparatus. They have never heard of Panini and Bhartrihari, or of Saussure, Sapir and Chomsky. Most of them were not aware of a great colonial scholar called George Abraham Grierson. To my mind, the modest value of the PLSI volumes lies precisely in the fact that this is not a work by linguists, or at least linguists alone, though some of the finest linguists of India have participated in the exercise and have guided its path. As the General Editor of the volumes, I hope, India will receive the 'snap shot of languages as they existed in the years 2011–12' posted here with affection, and write back to the team of hundreds who joined hands to make taking the snap shot possible with a warm 'Thank you... yours sincerely.' I look forward to conveying that appreciation to the large team of advisors, members of the National Editorial Collective and my colleagues in every state who participated in making the PLSI, who are too large in numbers to be named individually.

G. N. Devy
Chairperson, People's Linguistic Survey of India

Table I: Distribution of Indian Languages

	Assamese	Bengali	Bodo	Dogri	Gujarati	Hindi	Kannada	Kashmiri	Konkani	Maithili	Malayalam	Manipuri	Marathi	Nepali	Oriya	Punjabi	Sanskrit	Santali	Sindhi	Tamil	Telugu	Urdu	Total
Indian Linguistic Distribution	128	812	13	22	449	4,110	369	54	24	119	322	14	701	28	322	283	N	63	25	592	721	502	10000
Jammu & Kashmir	6	14	N	2,194	4	1,861	4	5,398	N	1	10	1	14	8	9	190	N	N	N	9	7	13	10000
Himachal Pradesh	1	8	N	31	5	8,929	1	83	N	3	2	N	3	116	7	601	N	N	N	2	2	8	10000
Punjab	1	8	N	7	3	760	2	1	N	1	4	N	5	8	4	9,170	N	N	N	5	3	11	10000
Chandigarh	3	61	N	10	38	6,760	5	19	1	14	26	4	15	60	17	2,792	N	N	1	64	15	81	10000
Uttaranchal	1	145	N	6	3	8,803	1	5	N	2	3	N	3	107	4	291	N	N	6	3	2	586	10000
																							10000
Haryana	1	19	N	1	3	8,734	1	2	N	6	7	N	4	10	5	1,057	N	N	3	5	3	123	10000
Delhi	5	151	N	5	33	8,100	8	15	1	62	66	1	19	32	21	715	N	N	31	67	20	632	10000
Rajasthan	N	10	N	1	10	9,109	1	N	N	1	6	N	3	2	2	202	N	N	67	2	2	117	10000
Uttar Pradesh	N	11	N	N	N	9,133	N	N	N	N	1	N	1	16	1	31	N	N	2	1	N	799	10000
Bihar	N	53	N	N	N	7,312	N	N	N	1,427	N	N	2	2	1	2	N	47	N	N	N	1,141	10000
																							10000
Sikkim	10	118	1	4	2	671	3	1	N	10	19	4	10	6,298	10	25	N	1	N	9	6	54	10000
Arunachal Pradesh	499	940	63	9	4	786	5	1	N	27	54	20	18	919	76	29	N	20	1	15	15	12	10000
Nagaland	93	326	27	3	3	315	2	N	N	4	22	38	8	189	22	8	N	1	N	8	7	4	10000
Manipur	7	130	N	3	1	118	1	N	N	2	6	6,067	2	220	4	7	N	1	N	11	3	2	10000
Mizoram	11	918	2	3	1	120	2	N	N	1	15	21	2	102	4	5	N	53	N	5	3	1	10000
																							10000
Tripura	4	6,735	N	2	4	168	2	N	N	1	5	65	3	11	75	5	–	8	N	4	12	1	10000
Meghalaya	158	804	15	2	1	217	1	N	N	2	9	15	167	226	5	21	N	2	1	4	2	11	10000
Assam	4,944	2,791	493	1	3	597	1	N	N	2	3	59	2	215	88	12	N	92	N	2	10	2	10000
West Bengal	1	8,534	5	N	6	717	N	N	N	3	2	N	2	128	23	8	N	280	1	3	26	206	10000
Jharkhand	N	969	N	N	7	5,765	N	N	N	52	3	N	5	6	174	32	N	1,070	1	5	13	864	10000
																							10000
Orissa	N	134	N	N	4	284	N	N	1	1	3	N	2	3	8,318	6	N	190	1	2	194	166	10000
Chhattisgarh	N	100	N	N	19	8,268	1	N	N	3	13	N	68	2	394	32	N	N	43	6	71	42	10000
Madhya Pradesh	N	17	N	1	33	8,732	1	N	N	N	8	N	210	2	3	25	N	N	43	4	4	197	10000
Gujarat	N	8	N	N	8,448	472	3	N	38	1	13	N	151	3	24	11	N	N	189	7	14	109	10000
Daman & Diu	17	116	N	1	6,883	1,977	25	1	15	24	75	1	435	90	133	20	1	4	14	22	19	37	10000
																							10000
Dadra & Nagar Haveli	6	63	N	–	2,371	1,513	33	N	1,038	36	84	N	528	47	82	13	–	2	6	30	28	45	10000
Maharashtra	N	32	N	N	239	1,104	130	1	68	4	42	N	6,889	7	10	28	N	N	73	55	145	713	10000
Andhra Pradesh	N	5	N	N	6	323	74	N	N	N	8	N	80	1	44	3	N	N	1	101	8,388	863	10000
Karnataka	N	8	N	N	19	256	6,626	N	146	N	133	N	360	2	3	3	N	N	3	357	703	1,054	10000
Goa	1	31	N	1	69	571	554	4	5,721	1	112	N	2,261	16	20	13	N	N	4	59	89	402	10000
																							10000
Lakshadweep	–	5	–	–	20	21	7	–	59	–	9,788	–	11	1	2	2	–	N	N	73	5	5	10000
Kerala	N	1	N	N	6	8	26	N	19	N	9,676	N	10	1	1	1	N	N	N	188	15	4	10000
Tamil Nadu	N	1	N	N	32	30	168	N	1	N	89	N	10	1	1	1	N	N	1	8,943	565	151	10000
Pondicherry	N	12	N	N	12	45	16	N	1	N	439	N	8	4	10	1	N	–	1	8,849	523	73	10000
Andaman & Nicobar Islands	2	2,595	N	1	11	1,840	9	N	1	2	818	1	37	22	25	52	–	2	N	1,784	1,293	46	10000

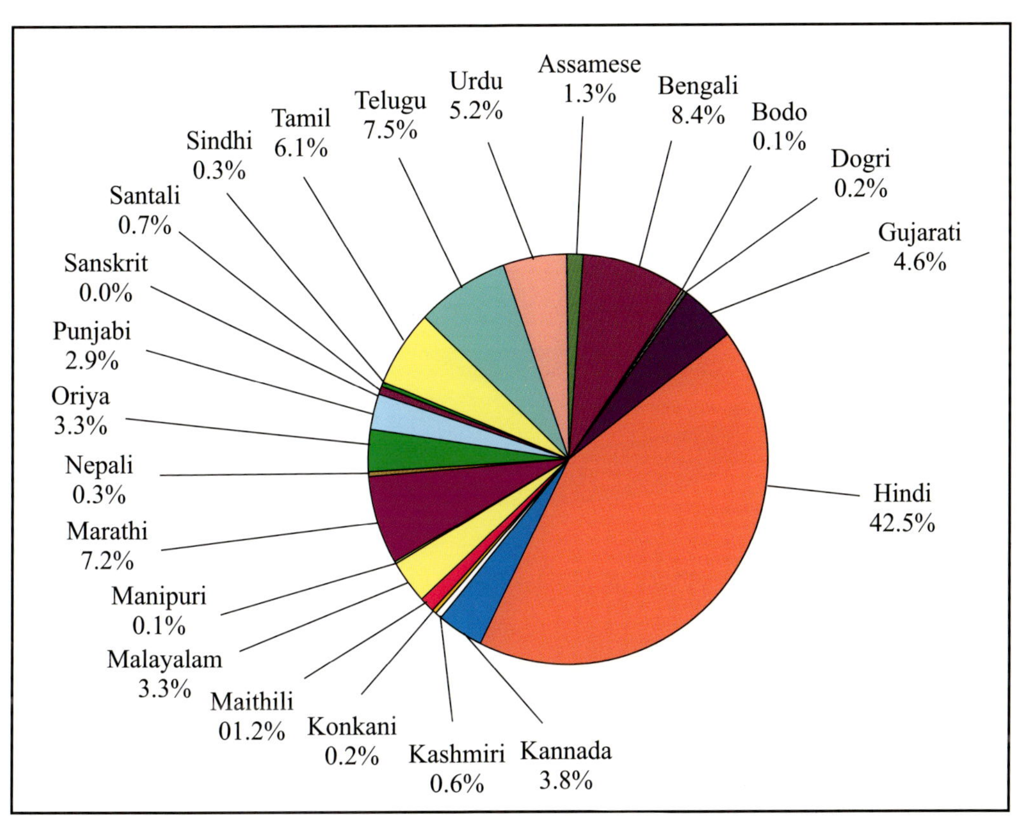

FIGURE I: DISTRIBUTION OF INDIAN LANGUAGES

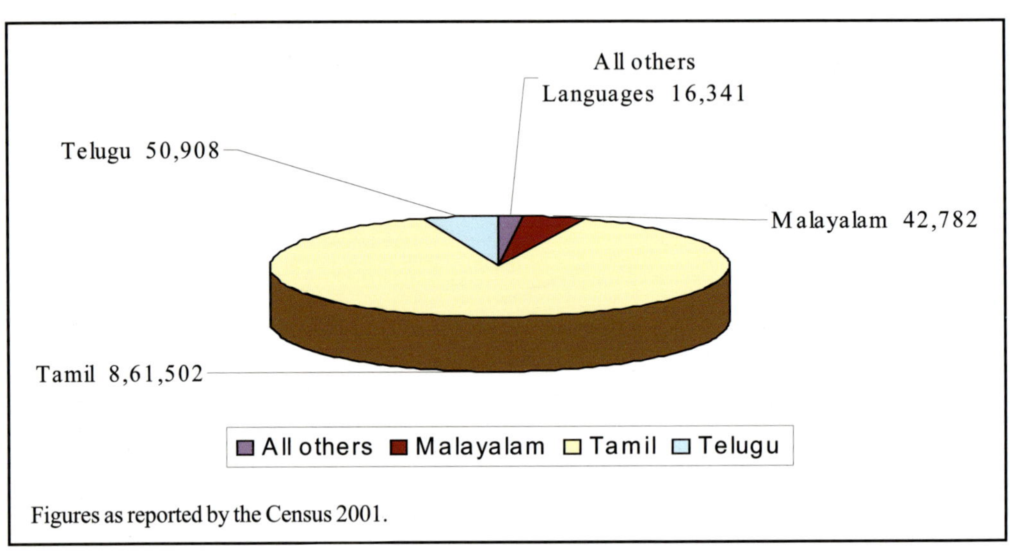

Figures as reported by the Census 2001.

FIGURE II: SPEAKERS OF SCHEDULED LANGUAGES IN PUDUCHERRY

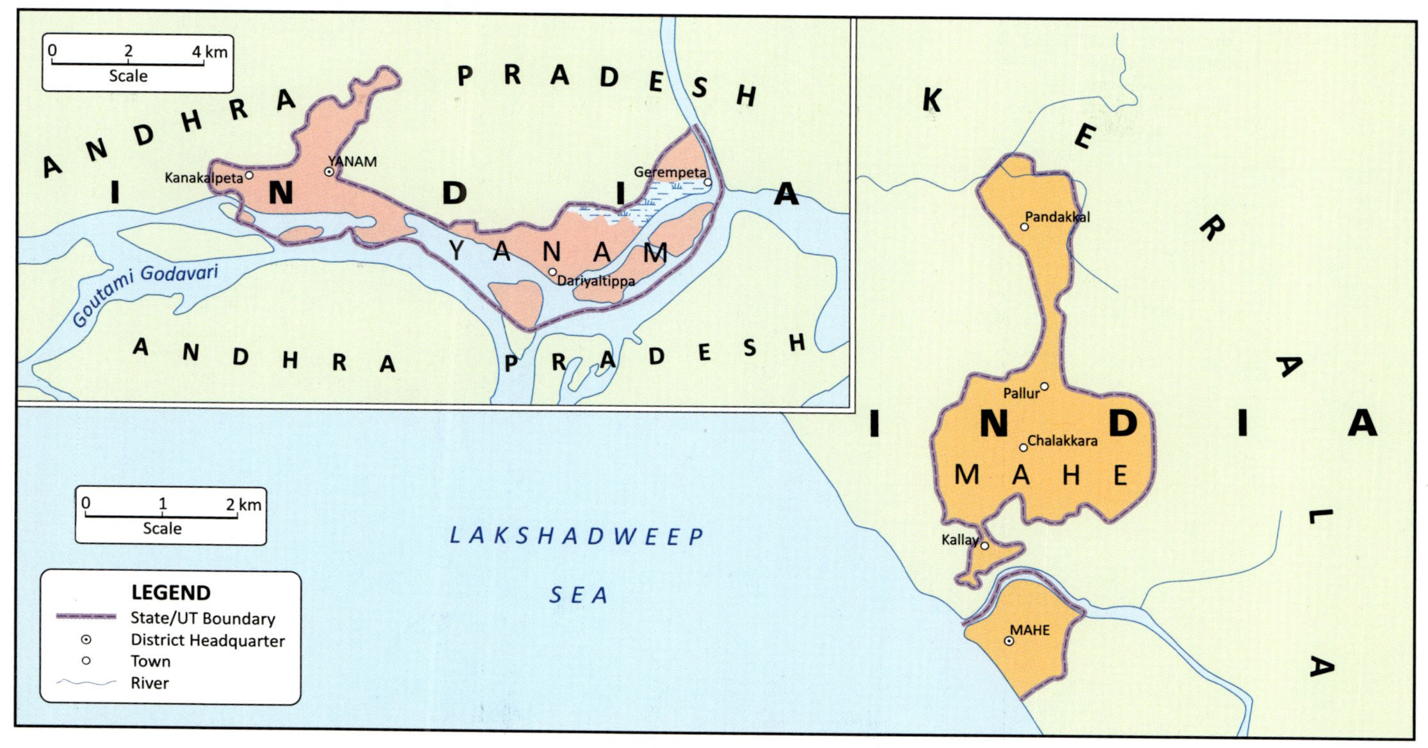

FIGURE III: MAP OF THE UNION TERRITORY OF PUDUCHERRY—PUDUCHERRY AND KARAIKAL

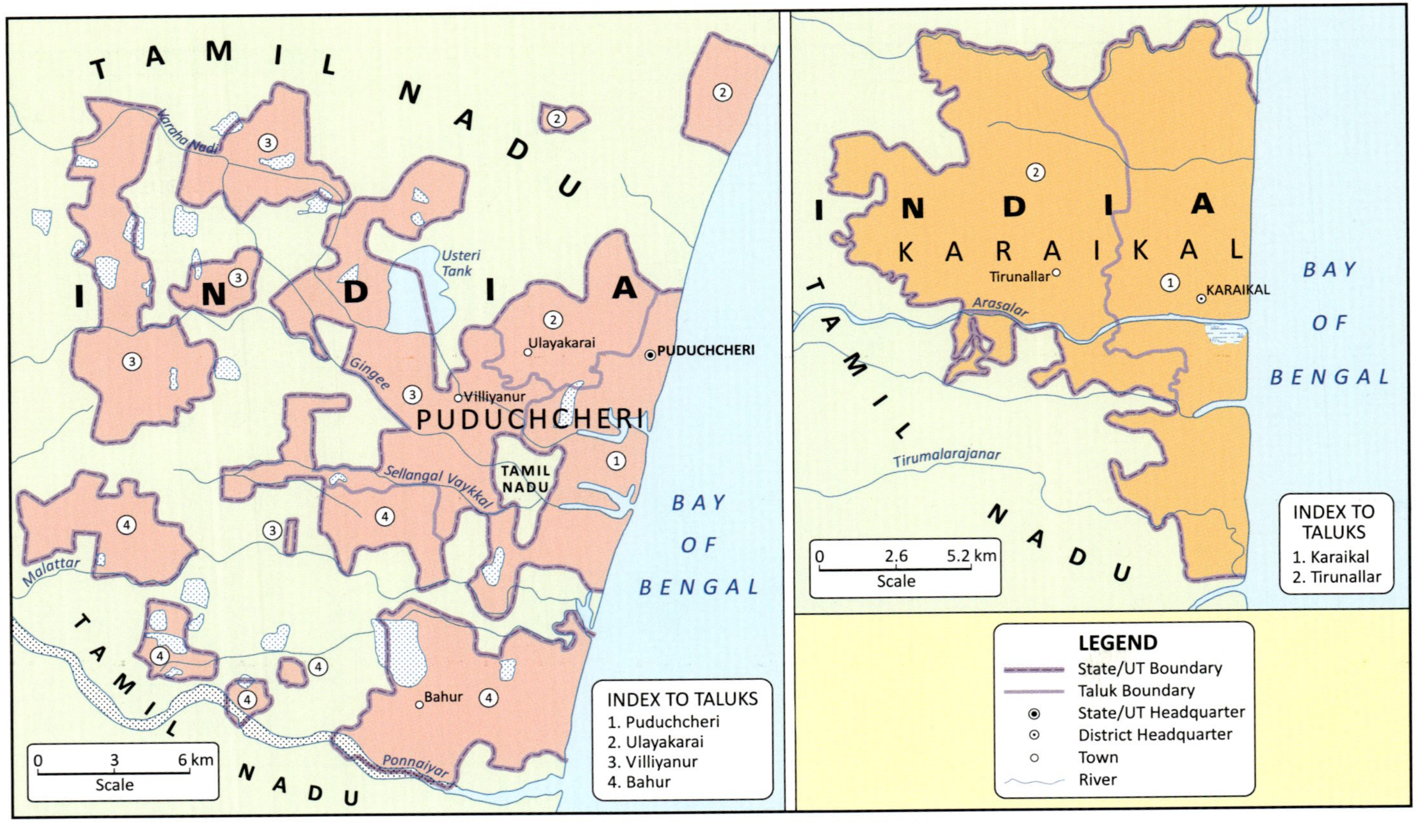

FIGURE IV: MAP OF THE UNION TERRITORY OF PUDUCHERRY—YANAM AND MAHE

Introduction to the Volume

The Puducherry volume of the *People's Linguistic Survey of India* (PLSI) is similar to other PLSI volumes in its representation as it is about the multiethnic, multicultural and multilingual nature of of Indian society. This is the characteristic feature of this small Union Territory of India. The four regions under this Union Territory have their own identity in terms of language, culture and even politics. Since the seventeenth century it was under French rule and has therefore deeply imbibed various elements of French culture and has adapted and localised the French language. It has experienced a continuous strife with the British, not to talk of the struggle for freedom by the people of Pondicherry. After its merger with the Indian Union in 1962, it has seen rapid development in all spheres. It stands out from the rest of the Indian states in education, industry, spirituality and politics. The language situation in Puducherry is unique as fifty-five languages were returned as the mother tongues of the population according to the 1961 Census. Nowhere in India did such a complexity of multilingualism exist. The four regions namely, Puducherry, Karaikal, Mahe and Yanam of this Union Territory which are geographically discontinuous have paved way for different policy decisions with regard to administration, education etc. Each region has its dominant language as the local official language. Tamil in Puducherry and Karaikal, Malayalam in Mahe and Telugu in Yanam. Still, English is used as the link language in all these regions of the Union Territory. The impact of French tradition can be seen in the life style of the people as well as in the landscape of Puducherry and in addition to the wider use of the French language among the inhabitants of these regions.

Another salient feature of the literary tradition of Puducherry is its contribution to the diary tradition. The history of Puducherry can be understood from the diaries written by Anandarangam Pillai and Thiruvenkatam Pillai who served as translators to French Governors. The spiritual identity of Puducherry has been well established by the Sri Aurobindo Ashram in the heart of Puducherry town. Since Puducherry was under French rule and as the population speaks different languages, the multilingual nature of Puducherry has raised, the awareness of linguistic purism among Tamils. Poets like Subramania Bharathi, Bharathidasan lived in Puducherry and contributed a lot to Tamil literature and poetics. This volume attempts to bring out the language situation of the Union Territory of Puducherry comprehensively and also its unique linguistic composition. It is the earnest hope of the editors of the volume the readers will get a glimpse of the sociolinguistic heritage of the Union Territory of Puducherry.

L. Ramamoorthy, G. Ravisankar
Editors

Contributors to the Volume

L. Ramamoorthy
Central Institute of Indian Languages
Mysore

G. Ravisankar
Puducherry Institute of Linguistics and Culture
Puducherry

An Appeal to Readers

In this volume we have covered the linguistic, literary and cultural aspects of Puducherry region alone. A comprehensive presentation on other areas like Mahe, Yanam, which are part of the union territory has been given and as has been mentioned elsewhere these as areas are geographically small and linguistically not so heterogeneous. Mahe forms part of Kerala and it adopts the language and education policy of Kerala. Yanam adopts the language policy of Andhra Pradesh. In these two parts the majority of the population speaks the dominant languages like Malayalam and Telugu.

Though the volume discusses at length themes like purism, language maintenance, language use, it has not directly dealt with languages other than Tamil, Telugu, Malayalam and French. There are no tribal language speakers in any significant numbers in the Puducherry Union Territory. However, if the readers wish to draw our attention to any such language for inclusion in a future edition of the volume, we shall gratefully consider such suggestions.

List of Languages Covered in this Volume

Tamil

Telugu

Malayalam

French

1

Introduction

PUDUCHERRY—GEOGRAPHICAL SPREAD

The Union territory of Puducherry comprises of four erstwhile French colonies, namely, Pondicherry, Karaikal, Mahe and Yanam. Pondicherry and Karaikal regions are embedded in the South Arcot and Thanjavur districts of Tamil Nadu respectively. Yanam is a small area encircled by the East Godavari district of Andhra Pradesh. Mahe is enclaved within the Kannur and Kozhikode districts in Kerala. Of these segments, the total area of Pondicherry alone is 293 square kilometre with a total population of 608388 (Census of India 1991). The 2001 Census is not available for Pondicherry.

The Pondicherry district is not a contiguous area. It is interspersed in the South Arcot District of Tamil Nadu. It is divided into two municipalities and six communes, having sixty-nine revenue villages. In a recent development, (2006) the Union Territory of Pondicherry has been officially renamed as the Union Territory of Puducherry. The name Puducherry is restricted to the district level, as Pondicherry district. The Pondicherry district which is under the Puducherry Union Territory is predominantly urban (66%). Three of its communes namely Bahour, Nettapakkam and Mannadipet are entirely rural while Ariankuppam and Villianur communes are predominantly rural and Ozhukarai, referred to in documents as Oulgaretpet, being almost entirely urban as is Pondicherry. In fact Pondicherry Urban Agglomeration consists of all the urban parts of Ariankuppam and Villianur besides all of Ozhukarai except a small pocket in the north. Pondicherry district may therefore be seen as consisting of an urban agglomeration with a rural hinterland which is interspersed and circumscribed by the rural South Arcot of Tamil Nadu which also serves as the hinterland of Puducherry. The population of the district is engaged mainly in services and manufacturing activities. But the communes vary considerably in this respect, with some population engaged in primary activities

While there is no variation in the proportion of workers understanding and speaking Tamil all over the district, there is a gap between the proportion of workers understanding and speaking English and other languages—the latter being less than the former. While the knowledge of English has spread across the district, knowledge of French is confined to the urban areas. So far as the use of Tamil at the workplace is concerned, the use of Tamil is more with subordinates than with superiors in all communes. From a sociolinguistic point of view more significant is that all over the districts except Mannadipet, the proportion of workers preferring to speak in Tamil is more with outsiders or strangers than with superiors, equals or subordinates.

Use of English at the workplace is more with superiors followed by equals and subordinates. The proportion of users of languages other than Tamil and English at the workplace is comparatively very small and with reference to the status of the interlocutor, slightly more with seniors as compared with juniors.

As pointed out earlier, there is a discrepancy in the knowledge and use of English at the workplace, especially with subordinates which is understandable, but the reasons for not using English with outsiders or strangers is not very clear. This discrepancy is maximum in Ozhukarai and minimum in the adjoining Villianur and Ariankuppam communes. The discrepancy in the knowledge and use of other languages is comparatively very less and not marked by much variation with reference to the status of the interlocutor.

There is a occupation-wise disparity in literacy skills (reading minus writing) in Tamil though Tamil is the preferred language at the workplace which indirectly suggests that Tamil is used more in interpersonal communication than in written communication. Obviously this disparity is more with people engaged in household activities. With regard to the main sectors of the economy, this disparity is more in the primary sector than in secondary or tertiary sectors. However communes vary in this regard.

Similarly, there are more number of people who can speak English or other languages than those who can write in them in the tertiary sector.

Language Composition of Puducherry

The territory has a very interesting language composition. An important feature of the 1961 Census was that as many as fifty-five Indian and foreign languages were returned as the mother tongues of the people in this small territory. Apart from all the eighteen official languages recognised by the Indian constitution, languages or dialects such as Bhojpuri, Coorgi (Kodava), Gorkhali, Konkani, Marwari, Parsi and European languages such as French, Portuguese, Irish, Polish and German also were recorded as the mother tongues of the population. Among other reasons, such diversity may have been due to three distinct linguistic areas. For example, Yanam is surrounded by Andhra Pradesh where Telugu is the dominant language, Mahe is surrounded by Kerala where Malayalam is the dominant language, and Pondicherry and Karaikal are surrounded by Tamil Nadu where the dominant language is Tamil.

The fact that several languages are spoken in the area, which comprises the Union Territory, has another historical explanation. South India witnessed waves of immigration of various races and castes for several centuries. Because of Pondicherry's long and close relation with Chandernagore in Bengal (a French Territory under colonial rule), and the existence of Sri Aurobindo Ashram, a good number of communities from the north and eastern states of India at different periods, such as Bengalis, Oriyas have settled down in Pondicherry. The close association of Pondicherry with the Maratha and Muslim rulers since seventeenth century introduced Urdu and Marathi into the territory. The Auroville, an International City, established by the devotees of The Mother has attracted many foreigners.

The Official Languages of Puducherry

The Pondicherry Official Language Act is also unique in its provisions: five languages, namely, Tamil, Telugu, Malayalam, English and French have been recognised for official purposes. The Official Language Act of the Union Territory states that Tamil shall be the language to be used for all or any of the official purposes of the Union Territory. In the case of Mahe, Malayalam may be used, and in the case of Yanam, Telugu may be used for all or any of the official purposes of the Union Territory. English may be used for all or any of the official purposes of the Union Territory. French shall remain the official language of establishments so long as the elected representatives of the people shall not decide otherwise (Act 28, Gazetteer, Pondicherry Vol.1 p. 911, The Pondicherry Official Language Act 1965 No.3 of 1965 *La Gazette de L'Etat de Pondichéry,* No.13).

According to the 2001 Census, the number of speakers for each official language is as follows:

Tamil:	220,749 (Puducherry and Karaikal district only)
Telugu:	31,362 (Yanam district only)
Malayalam:	38,823 (Mahe district only)
French:	above 10,000

Even though the Official Language Act of Pondicherry recognises Tamil, Telugu, Malayalam and French, most of the official transaction is carried out in English. The earlier records in the registrar offices and municipalities were maintained in French. Due to the scattered geographical nature of the Union Territory in Kerala and Andhra Pradesh, the use of English is not dispensed with.

The Government of Puducherry has created a Tamil Development Cell to promote the use of Tamil for official purposes. Even then, the switch over from English to Tamil has not been completed just as we notice in Tamil Nadu. One may conjecture that this transition will be neiher smooth nor quick.

Bilingualism in Puducherry

Apart from the languages included in the Eighth Schedule of the Constitution of India, many minor languages are also spoken in Puducherry. In addition to the mother tongues, residents of the Union Territory demonstrate in their daily activities, significant knowledge of other tongues. This multilingualism is a widely prevalent phenomenon. It can be said that almost all minority speakers, except a few people in Sri Aurobindo Ashram, know Tamil as it is the dominant language of the region.

One interesting aspect in Puducherry is that even a monolingual Hindi or Bengali speaker can live in the Ashram area without learning Tamil. Perhaps the reason is that the Ashram is run mostly by Bengalis. English is the sole contact language for Aurovilleans. However, it is not unusual in India that there exist areas or locations, where the dominant regional language is not known to all the residents of those areas or locations.

Each language group knows other languages by virtue of the environment of schooling. The languages known to each mother tongue group as given in 1981 Census is tabulated below. Only major languages known to significant strength of population are identified for this purpose.

Mother tongue		Other languages known in decreasing order of strength
Assamese	(A)	Bengali
Bengali	(B)	B E H Ta
Gujarati	(G)	G –E- Ta – H =Skt – B
Hindi	(H)	H –E Ta – G – P – U – u
Kannada	(K)	Ka, Ta – E – H
Malayalam	(M)	M – Ta – E – H -
Marathi	(M)	Ma – T – E – H
Odia	(O)	O – E _ G – Ta
Punjabi	(P)	P – E – H – Ta
Sindhi	(S)	S – E – H – Ta
Tamil	(Ta)	Ta – E – Te – H - U
English	(E)	E – Ta – H
Telugu	(Te)	Te – Ta – E – H
Urdu	(U)	U – Ta – E – H

Subramaniyan (1997:28) states that the measure of known language by the members of a speech community is an indicator of *language load,* carried by the community. In Puducherry, for every speech community, the language load is certainly high because of the multilingual set up.

The fourteen mother tongue groups listed in the above table may be classified into two broad groups: The first one is people with the knowledge of Hindi and English for preferred or high performance, and the second one is people with knowledge of Tamil and English for preferred or high performance. Speakers of languages such as Bengali, Gujarati, Hindi, Odia, Punjabi and Sindhi use Hindi and English as the dominant language next to their mother tongue. But, for other language groups such as Telugu, Kannada, Marathi and Urdu, it is Tamil and English which are known to the majority of speakers, next to their mother tongue. It is a unique diversification observable in Puducherry.

Other languages	Percentage to total speakers of particular languages		
	Tamil	English	Hindi
Bengali	4.18	58.46	19.19
Gujarati	27.3	41.8	14.5
Hindi	29.5	33.2	-
Kannada	54.3	26.8	1.5
Malayalam	5.8	21.1	1.3
Marathi	54.6	20.6	5.8
Odia	3.16	44.9	25.9

Punjabi	3.4	54.6	30.2
Sindhi	2.5	50	10.3
Telugu	39.2	7.4	4.6
Urdu	60	8.1	1.8

The percentage of people with knowledge of Hindi, English and Tamil shows very interesting results. Among north and east Indian languages, in Bengali, Odia, Sindhi and Punjabi speech communities, the percentage of Tamil knowing population ranges from 2.5%–4.1% only. But, in the case of Gujarati and Hindi groups, the percentage of Tamil knowledge is higher, which ranges from 27–29% Among the Marathi and Urdu mother tongue group, more than fifty per cent of the population knows Tamil. as is the case of people belonging to other parts of south India.

Among the south Indian language speakers the Kannada mother tongue group in Puducherry, i.e., 54.3% has knowledge of Tamil. But, in the case of Telugu and Malayalam, the percentage is lower than that of the Kannada group among the minority speakers in the Union Territory. This is because there are separate pockets where Malayalam and Telugu mother tongue groups occupy the majority position.. But the percentage of Tamil knowing population in these groups is less than that of Kannada mother tongue group. This is mainly due to the separate geographical locations like Mahe and Yanam regions where the majority of the population is monolingual in Malayalam and Telugu with very few bilinguals. Similarly, the percentage of people who know English is high among those whose mother tongue is Bengali, Gujarati, Punjabi or Sindhi.

Hindi knowing people are high among Odia and Punjabi language groups. It is interesting to note the low percentage of Hindi knowing people and high percentage of Hindi and English knowing people in some mother tongue groups like Bengali, Odia and Punjabi. It may be worth observing that the present generation whose mother tongue is Bengali, Gujarati and even Odia, have attained proficiency in Tamil as far as Pondicherry district is concerned, in addition to their respective mother tongues.

The Mother has said,"…There should be somewhere on earth, a place that no nation can claim as the sole property; a place where all human beings of goodwill, sincere in their aspiration, could live freely as citizens of the world, obeying one single authority, that of the supreme Truth, a place of peace concord, harmony..."

This vision of the Mother is realised as Auroville, 'the city of dawn', on the outskirts of Puducherry in the territory of Tamil Nadu. A person can get over his racial, religious and cultural prejudices if he lives in Auroville. Though this is true for the people of Auroville, it has a paramount impact on the socio-cultural life of the people of Puducherry. The existing patterns of multilingualism and multiculturalism in Puducherry, can be said to be as the by-products of Auroville and the Ashram. Even before the establishment of the Ashram, the culture of Pondicherry was nurtured by French ideology, viz., equality, liberty and fraternity that facilitated the development of multilingualism and multiculturalism. Having remained as the capital of erstwhile French India for nearly 138 years, the legacies of Pondicherry has a special flavour that is not found anywhere in the Indian sub-continent. French influence is evident in the realms of language, dress, food, music, architecture, arts and crafts and even in matters of customs and conventions. Although the vast majority of the people in Puducherry are bound by Indian cultural tradition, a good number of people who have some kind of link with France or the French people are still open to French cultural influence.

Socio-Cultural History of Puducherry

Puducherry has a very long socio-cultural history that can be traced back to the Sangam period through the evidences in Tamil literature and the trade relation it had with the Romans and the Greeks. These facts have evidence in the archeological excavation in Arikamedu near Puducherry. The non-linguistic items such as pottery, vessels, coins etc., excavated from the site may throw more light on the socio- cultural life of the people of that period. But our concern here is the study of linguistic landscaping items that have social and cultural significance in modern Puducherry. Linguistic Landscape (LL) according to Landry and Bourhis (1997:23–43) refer to all linguistic objects, which mark the public area.

The Union Territory of Puducherry is the creation of Seventh Amendment of Indian Constitution. The role of the Government of India is predominant in shaping the LL of Union Territories. For the territories, which are politically and linguistically influenced by the adjacent states, the mother tongue taking an exclusive policy for them is very difficult. This is very much evident from the experiences of Puducherry with regard to administrative and educational policies. The fluidity of policies may be due to the pressures of dominant linguistic group and minority population. In this background, the linguistic landscape code with respect to the domains of education and administration and the reflections of LL on the socio-cultural life of Puducherry and the role of the government and others in this context can very well be analysed. The LL items selected here include personal names, street names and other official documents.

Demography

The total area of Union Territory of Puducherry is 492 square kilometre. Total household population is 5,99,384. The major languages are: Tamil in Puducherry and Karaikal, Malayalam in Mahe and Telugu in Yanam.

Major Linguistic Minority Population

(1% or more of the states household population)

Eighth Schedule Language Speakers

Malayalam	30,886 (5.15%)
Telugu	24,114 (4.02%)

Minor Linguistic Minority Population

(0.10% to 0.99% of the states household population)

Eighth Schedule Language Speakers

Gujarati	786 (0.13%)
Hindi	1,381 (0.23%)
Kannada	689 (0.11%)
Urdu	4,176 (0.70%)

Microscopic Linguistic Minority Population

(Less than 0.10% of the state household population)

Eighth Schedule Languages speakers

Bengali	547	(0.09%)
Kashmiri	8	-
Marathi	409	(0.07%)
Oriya	94	(0.02%)
Punjabi	67	(0.01%)
Sindhi	62	(0.01%)
Others		
Arabic	22	
English	339	(0.06%)
Gorkhali	198	(0.03%)
Konkani	29	
Korwa	01	
Tibetan	45	(0.01%)
Telugu	24	

Rest of languages 1022 (0.17%)

(Figures based on the 1981 Census)

The Status of Minority Languages

According to the report, there are no recognised linguistic minority groups in the territory, since none of the minority language speakers constitute fifteen per cent or more of the local population in any of the regions. In view of the absence of any recognised linguistic minority in the territory the question of publication of rules in minority languages does not arise. Tamil, Malayalam, Telugu, English and French are the recognised media of instruction in the territory. However, no orders exist for providing instruction through minority languages.

In the Union Territory of Puducherry, among the minority languages, Malayalam occupies the first position in terms of the numerical strength of its speakers. The second largest minority language is Telugu.

Year	Union Territory of Puducherry	(Pondicherry)
1971	17,413	8,438
1981	24,114	12,461

Almost half of the Telugu speaking population of the Union Territory lives in Puducherry. . The commune-wise population of Telugu minority community as recorded in 1971 and 1981 censuses are given below:

Commune	1971	1981
Pondicherry	2,938	6,032

Ariankuppam	245	539
Oulgaret	737	1,842
Mannadipet	1,218	1,616
Bahour	652	602
Villianoor	685	678
Nettapakkam	809	1,152

From the table above, we note that the Telugu speaking population decreases in Bahour and Villianoor Communes. The rate of growth of population is not proportionate to the Telugu mother tongue population. In other communes, there is a steady increase in the population growth, which shows that the language is still maintained in those communes. The major languages spoken in Puducherry are Tamil, Malayalam and Telugu. According to 1981 census, within 2348 households in Puducherry alone, 12,461 people are Telugu speakers. But on the whole, 24,114 people speak Telugu in the Union Territory of Puducherry.

Multilingualism in Puducherry

In spite of the re-organisation of Indian states in 1956 on linguistic basis, we can find the presence of more than two languages of other states as minority languages in every state. But in the case of Puducherry, the language situation is peculiar and unique. It is to be mentioned that fifty-five Indian and foreign languages were returned as the mother tongue of the population in the 1961 census. Within the small area of 492 square kilometre, with a population of 8.07 lakhs (according to the 1981 census), the existence of these many languages is strange. The thirtieth report of the commission for linguistic minorities also classified the available Indian languages—Tamil, Malayalam, Telugu, Gujarati, Hindi, Kannada, Urdu, Bengali, Kashmiri, Marathi, Odia, Punjabi, and Sindhi—under major and minor languages. The complexity of languages in Puducherry makes it a miniature of Indian multilingual set up.

Scholars opine that the existence and maintenance of diversity, whether cultural, linguistic, or religious, have always been a part of the Indian tradition. Apart from this Indian tradition, there are some other factors which are responsible for the convergence of people from different backgrounds to Puducherry. The establishment of Auroville and Sri Aurobindo Ashram may be one of the prime factors as mentioned in the beginning of this chapter. The other major factors may be because of the disjointed nature, at least geographically, of the constituents of the Union Territory of Puducherry and French colonialism.

The Union Territory of Puducherry comprises four erstwhile French establishments., Pondicherry, Karaikal, Mahe and Yanam. The regions of Mahe and Yanam are closer to Kerala and Andhra Pradesh respectively and Pondicherry and Karaikal to Tamil Nadu. Naturally, the dominant languages of these respective states are the dominant languages in these pockets. These pockets also reflect the multilingual character of the adjacent states to a certain extent.

The other important factor for the multilingual landscape in Puducherry is French colonialism. While all other Indian states were under British rule, these pockets were colonies of the French. French ideologies might have attracted many people to Pondicherry as political refugees and for purposes of business. With such multilingual patterns in Puducherry, the following sections focus on the linguistic landscape in various domains and the role of the government and others in shaping the language loyalty (LL).

Language Loyalty (LL) and Administration

The language of administration in a multilingual set up has a great role to play, particularly because, none of the minority language speakers constitute more than ten per cent of the total population of the region. Among the minority languages, Malayalam occupies the first position in terms of the numerical strength of its speakers. The second largest minority language is Telugu. The official language policies are framed in the Union Territory also keeping in view its geographical discontinuity.

The official language document of the Union Territory states that Tamil should be the language for all or any of the official purposes of the Union Territory. In the case of Mahe and Yanam, Malayalam and Telugu respectively may be used for official purposes. English may also be used for all or any of the official purposes. French shall remain the official language of the establishment as long as the elected representatives of the people do not decide otherwise. (Act 28, Gazetteer, Pondicherry Vol. 1, p. 11 Pondicherry Official Language Act 1965, Act 3). Before the de facto transfer of the UTP, it was French that was used for all official purposes. After the transfer of the UTP to India, English has acquired the place of pride. Nevertheless, traces of French administration are still felt in Pondicherry as far as municipal administration is concerned. The French division of communes continues for administrative purposes, though the revenue division of Pondicherry is different.

The use of English instead of Tamil for all official purposes underscores the inconsistent LL code with regard to administration. In the government even though the official language policy states that Tamil should be used for official purposes, it is not at all followed by the government. All correspondences to the public are only in English. The role of the Action Committee for Tamil Development (ACTD) with respect to LL in administration must be mentioned here. It is an organisation mostly of Tamil teachers and scholars whose aims are to protect Tamil from the dominance of other languages and to make Tamil as an administrative language and medium of instruction. Due to their untiring efforts, the administration started using Tamil to a limited extent. One of the LL acts by ACTD is that it succeeded in forcing the government to issue notice advising all officials to put their signature in Tamil. But the government does not follow even that memorandum properly. The government favours English as the language of power though of a minority, but the ACTD's concerns are towards that of the majority.

Another LL item of the government's inconsistency is with reference to its order in the use of the very name 'Puducherry'. The old name of Puducherry was Pondicherry and the French administration used this name in the beginning for its official purpose. A newcomer to Puducherry may be confused on seeing the name board in the buses. Most of the buses use the name Pondy as a simplified form of Pondicherry. The Tamil groups, through demonstrations and representations, pleaded with the government and public to use 'Puducherry' instead of Pondicherry. They even conducted demonstrations against the newspapers which use Pondicherry and burnt the copies of the Tamil newspaper *Dinamalar.* The government also passed orders with due approval of the assembly pending the approval of the Central Government to use Puducherry in all places. But that order was followed neither by the government nor by the public. The government uses 'Puducherry' in the Tamil correspondences and in its transport corporation. But when it is written in English, 'Pondicherry' is used. The issue of using the appropriate name for the UTP was raised in the state assembly a few years ago and the then chief minister clarified that the district and the Union Territory will be referred to as 'Puducherry' and the old town under French rule will be referred to as 'Pondicherry' which was not acceptable to certain political parties. The issue remains unresolved even today and the inconsistency continues to exist.

Language Loyalty (LL) and Education

The LL with respect to education in Puducherry is as varied as in the case of administration, although for different reasons. The Union Territory of Puducherry does not have a policy of education of its own. Depending upon the geographical location of its constituents, the territory adopts the policies of the adjacent states. As far as school education is concerned, the territory is considered to be a part of the respective states such as Tamil Nadu, Kerala and Andhra Pradesh. The examination is also conducted by these states for Puducherry students. The attempts to form a separate educational board for Puducherry have not materialised yet.

The Union Territory of Puducherry follows two different policies with respect to language education viz., three language formula for Mahe and Yanam regions as adopted by Kerala and Andhra Pradesh and a two language formula for Puducherry and Karaikal region as followed by Tamil Nadu. Hence Tamil, Telugu, Malayalam are studied as first language in the respective regions. English is the second language. Mahe and Yanam regions have Hindi from class 5, irrespective of the medium of instruction.

However, the situation in urban Puducherry is complex and unique. Urban Pondicherry has remnants of French rule in education. French is introduced in school curriculum along with Tamil or Hindi both by government and private schools. The number of languages introduced and the manner of introduction (such as optional or compulsory) and the level of introduction vary from school to school.

One interesting situation in Puducherry is that Tamil, Hindi and French are being taught as first languages in the school curriculum. One can select any one of the languages in school and can change the first language option at the secondary and higher secondary stages. Hence, even without learning Tamil, the dominant language of the region, one can finish school education.

The LL and education are in a state of confrontation with respect to the policies of private and government schools. Making of Tamil, Hindi, and Sanskrit as compulsory or optional languages differs from schools to school.

It is to be noted that the other official languages, Malayalam and Telugu are not taught in the school curriculum in urban Pondicherry and similarly Tamil is not taught in Mahe and Yanam. The important LL with respect to education is that French is retained in schools as optional even though it has been totally replaced by English in administration. French in Puducherry is not only a vestige of the past, but also used as a link language to establish future ties with France. When the French quit during 1956, they established an institute, Alliance Française to ensure their cultural continuity. They also established Lycee Français a French school where French is the medium of instruction. The Puducherry Government also established French medium schools and made provision to study French at BA, and MA all levels at colleges and in the university. There are also institutes like Ecole Française, D'Extreme Orient and Institut Français which give unique status to Puducherry as research centres established by the French Government.

The interests of the government and the private schools to continue the French language as a medium are different. In the case of the former it is to ensure the continuation of its cultural heritage while in the case of the latter it is to enable the students to score high marks and find better employment opportunities in France.

As far LL in education is concerned, the government does not have a uniform policy to be followed by all schools. Moreover it has no control over the policies of private schools. Puducherry, being an Union Territory, the government adopts the policy of the centre and at the same time yields to the pressure of the dominant Tamil group which itself is influenced by the ideology of Tamil Nadu, i.e., opposition to the imposition of Hindi. So far, we have seen the remnants of French and the linguistic landscaping in the domains of education and administration. There are other items of linguistic landscaping such as personal names and street names in Puducherry, which also show the relics of French culture.

Language Loyalty (LL) and Personal Names

Personal names constitute an important source for the study of the social, religious, and linguistic aspects of a society. In the case of the Puducherry Union Territory, due to its scattered location, multilingual and multiethnic composition, one would find a lot of interesting aspects in the study of personal names. There are three types of names that have landscaping relevance among the people of Pondicherry. They are 1. Names with patronymic titles 2. Names with French spelling 3. Pure Tamil names with titles.

There is a group of people who have patronymic names in Puducherry. They are all natives of Pondicherry and renounced their personal status during French colonial period. They are called *Reno cants.* According to a French decree, *Reno cants* after attaining the age of twenty-one had to adopt a patronymic name which was to be passed on to their descendents Any person in, a French colony in India, irrespective of caste, creed or colour, could enjoy the rights and privileges of French citizenship by adopting a special patronymic name. They constitute a separate ethnic group who have a new culture, which is a blend of both Tamil and French cultures. There are also people with patronymic names without French citizenship in Puducherry. They are the people who failed to opt for French nationality in 1954 (legally 1962 i.e. on, during the defacto transfer of Pondicherry but still keep the names due to the renunciations made by their forefathers. The patronymic names are of different kinds. (See for details Jayaraj Daniel, PJDS 1:1, 1991) These patronymic names are best examples to show the blend of two cultures.

Example Paume Manickme

Bala Gourou Radjagobalan

Le Berger Antoine

By seeing the name, one can understand the identity of these people in Puducherry. The second type of linguistic landscape is the names with French spelling. There is a group of Puducherry citizen whose names are written in French spelling in the records, example, Selvaradjou, Doressamy, Aroquiadasse, Pandourangane.

These tokens are also the relics of the impact of the French language. Most of the people whose names are written in French spelling are middle aged and older. Even without having French citizenship or connections or even knowledge of French language, some people write their names with a French spelling. This spelling system is not an adoption by them but a kind of imposition on the people by the then French knowing officials.

These LL tokens indicate the status of French in those days. The French language was the language of administration, law, medium of education in Puducherry. Even after Independence, the administration continued to use French until English took over its place. This is because most of the municipal administrators and other officials were educated through French medium. When they were in charge of recording the birth of a child in municipalities they wrote the names in French spelling. There is a provision in the Official Language Act that French shall remain the official language as long as the elected representatives of the people shall not decide otherwise. But English has replaced French because of the inter-state and central communications whose medium is in English in Puducherry.

The third type of personal names is Tamil names with titles. These LL tokens used by the Tamil purists are as important as the French personal names. There is a trend among the Tamil school teachers and Tamil scholars, either to change their name after a pure Tamil name or to add some kind of a title before their names.

Example Subramaniyan–Thirumurugan

Natarajan–Kuttarasan

There are also some titles conferred by literary associations to honour particular individuals as follows:

Illakkanacutar, Kavimani, Kambavanar, Ellucippavalar

The government also confers titles to literary personalities such as Tamilmaamani, Kalaimaamani, Telugu Ratna, Malayala Ratna for their services rendered to literature. Such types of acts by the puritans are purely identity related acts due to the impact of the pure Tamil movement in Tamil Nadu. Their overt ideology by such acts is to protect Tamil and Tamil culture from the domination of other languages and cultures. The puritans also name their children and houses after pure Tamil names and advise others to do so. In order to facilitate the public to use Tamil names for their children they put up boards in the street corners near government hospital with a list of Tamil names. The actions of the puritans and the Action Committee for Tamil Development have to be viewed in a broad socio-cultural context in order to understand these types of LLs. The interesting aspects of the group is that they do not try to change French names, or correct French spelling which violate the grammatical tradition of Tamil. Their acts are directed towards Sanskrit and other names.

Language Loyalty (LL) and Street Names

The street names in Puducherry are another significant linguistic landscaping item providing information about the presence of social and linguistic groups and their power relation. The relics of French rule are still felt in every aspect of Puducherry such as city planning, roads, houses etc. The city is constructed in such a way that well planned streets run from east to west and north to south in a perfect rectangle. A long canal that runs from north to south was constructed to separate the white people from non-whites. The separation of geographical landscape is reinforced with the linguistic landscape also. Goffman's (1973) statement that the linguistic token and label on the street makeup—the markers of geographical territories as well as social boundaries—is true in the case of earlier Pondicherry. The settlements were made on the basis of caste, religion and occupation in the town; the powerful group occupied the centre of the city and around temples; the weavers and business communities formed the next layer, Muslims and others were located at the outskirt of the city (Arokianathan, 1990 and Sebastian 1999). This is very much evident from the names of the streets and its location such as Vellalar Street, Chetty Street, Vysial Street, Vannaratteru, Kandappa Mudaliar Street, Chinna Subbaraya Pillai Street, Hajiyar Street, Milad Viti, Thillai Mestri Viti etc. The street names not only portray the settlement of different castes but also indicate the status of languages also. At present three types of street name boards are used in Puducherry. They are:

(1) French-Tamil bilingual boards

(2) Tamil-English bilingual boards

(3) Tamil monolingual boards

The French-Tamil bilingual boards are earlier version of the boards that were put up by the Government of Pondicherry. In these boards the names are written in white letters on blue metal plates.

They are fixed on the walls of the house at the beginning of every street. The name of the street is written in French on the top, and in Tamil next to French. This clearly indicates the status of French in those days and even after the Independence. It is to be noted that the streets in the white town are mostly named after French Governors or other personalities. The streets are still called by these names in the white city without any change even now.

Example Rue Victor Simovel, Rue Suffren, Rue Monthesier, Rue Morasin, Rue Orlean Rue Laporth etc.

The second types of boards are Tamil-English bilingual boards erected during later days. These cement boards are yellow in colour and the names are written in black letters. They are placed on the side of the boards of every street. The names are written in Tamil first and then in English, which reflects the status of Tamil nowadays. These boards are found in all streets of the part of the city which were inhabited by the Indian population and a few in the areas occupied by the whites. The names are given after temples, caste, and political leaders.

Example Muthu Mariamman Koil Street, Easwaran Koil Street, Cathedral Street, Chetty Street, Vysial Street, Nehru Street, Mahatma Gandhi Street, Vallabhai Patel Street etc.

Some streets named after the French personalities and caste were replaced in later days indicating the social changes taking place.

Example Rue Dupleix has been renamed to Nehru Street

Kosakadi viti is now Ambalathadaiyar Viti

Chinna Paparaviti has been replaced with Savorirayalau Street

Itaiyar teru is now known as—Pillai Street

Rue Bussy has been changed—Lal Bahadur Shastri Street

Even though the names are changed, one can find the old names in French plates and the sign boards of private commercial establishments and in the speech of the people.

Example

Rue Cathedral–Mada kovil teru

The third types of street names are Tamil boards that appear in the extension areas. The newly developed areas are named after Tamil poets, Tamil political leaders etc.

Example Anna Nagar, Thantai Periyar Nagar, Bharathidasan Nagar, Nanbargal Nagar, Kamban Nagar, Thiruvalluvar Nagar, Tagore Nagar etc.

Tamil identity and love of Tamil literateurs are expressed in the naming of boards by the Tamil people. The street names in Puducherry show changing status of languages, French, English and Tamil. It also indicates the social changes taking place. The government's act with regard to using Tamil and English in boards is to facilitate the multilingual population and tourists.

References

Daniel, Jeyaraj. 1991.' A study of patronymic names of Tamil *renocants* of Pondicherry'. *PJDS*,1/1, 57–58.

Landry, R. and R. Y. Bourhis. 1997. 'Linguistic landscape and ethnolinguistic vitality: An empirical study'. *Journal of Language and Social Psychology*, 16/1, 23–49.

Subramanian, V. I. 1997. 'Exploring the causes for the preservation/loss of languages in India.' *IJDL*, 36/2.

2

Tamil

BILINGUAL SITUATION AMONG THE SPEAKERS OF TAMIL IN PUDUCHERRY

The actual language use situation will be much more helpful in working out the linguistic profile of Puducherry. However, before studying the domains of actual use of languages, the bilingual situation in the majority language, namely, Tamil, may be analysed using the 1981 Census figures.

Language	Percentage to total Tamil Population
English	16.9%
Telugu	0.7%
Hindi	0.15%
Urdu	0.12%
Malayalam	0.07%
Kannada	0.1% (less than)

India is a multilingual and multicultural country. There is hardly any region in India where only one regional language is understood and spoken. The small Union Territory of Puducherry is no exception. It is unique as it recognises two foreign and three regional languages as the official state languages. These are Tamil, Telegu, Malayalam, English and French. An interplay of historical, political and cultural factors is at the root of such a situation. A brief recapitulation of these factors would not be out of place before we discuss different aspects of Tamil, the language spoken by a majority in the Union Territory.

Till 1956, Pondicherry and Karaikal in Tamil Nadu, Yanam in Andhra Pradesh and Mahe in Kerala were under French rule (as were many other parts of India under the British till 1947). After the French ceded their colonies and these regions were integrated within the Indian Union, the Government of India recognised the three regional languages and both the languages of the colonial masters. Thus the scattered nature of the French territories on both the east and west coast of peninsular India prompted the Government of India to accept the languages spoken by a maximum number of people in the region.

Such a decision has manifold purposes. As in other states that were reorganised on the basis of linguistic majority of the population, the Government of India continued and promoted the multilingual and multicultural traditions of this country. Moreover, post-Independence, English was recognised and accepted as the link language which also threw open both education and job opportunities all over India and abroad. As for French, there were many people in this erstwhile French colony who had opted for French citizenship. Not only the government of France but also that of India, retained and offered French as a medium of interaction in urban Puducherry. It was also stated in the Pondicherry Official Language Act that the 'French language shall remain the official language of establishments so long as the elected representatives of the people shall not decide otherwise.' (Act 28, Gazetteer, Pondicherry, vol. I, p. 911 as quoted in *Language in India—Strength for Today and Bright hope for Tomorrow* vol. 10; January 2012).

Moreover the presence of Sri Aurobindo Ashram and Auroville (near Puducherry) supported the promotion of a varied and diverse official language policy.

In this chapter, we shall focus on Tamil which is spoken by approximately 89% of the population. This is because Puducherry and Karaikal regions are surrounded by South Arcot and Thanjavur districts of Tamil Nadu. Hence, Tamil is the language of the majority of the local population.

The antiquity of Tamil language is unquestionable. The Sangam literature of third century BC establishes the existence of the languages for long. One of the recognised classical language, Tamil was used in ancient periods to carve on inscriptions, to record philosophical and moral discourses and official decrees. The situation changed with the arrival of the Europeans who subjugated different parts of peninsular India to set up their own colonies. It was only after the Independence from the colonial rulers that Tamil was recognised as the medium of instruction in schools and colleges (along with English and French), and was accepted as the language of administration, judiciary and mass-media—language domains where French and English had hitherto played key roles. The retention of both English and French along with three vernacular languages of the south sought to facilitate a slow and gradual changeover and thereby prevent abrupt disruption in day-to-day administrative activities. It was, however, envisaged by the Government of the Union Territory that Tamil would be studied by all the school-going population of the eastern coast of the peninsula. But the ground reality is somewhat different and we shall come back to the prevalent current situation in a later section.

Characteristics of Tamil Language before the advent of European Missionaries

As in all other regional languages of India, oral verse form preceded the written prose form. The progress from oracy to literacy was slow and gradual. Sanskrit was the language of religions scriptures, literature, philosophical treatise etc. Not only in northern India but also down south, the influence of Sanskrit was supreme. As education was restricted to an elite few (mostly Brahmins), knowledge of Sanskrit was restricted. And not surprisingly, in a bid to retain their social influential position, the elite class was not keen to share their knowledge with others. They were the ones who held all important jobs and positions.

The influence of Sanskrit on Tamil literature was significant. The *manipra:vala* style or the practice of using Sanskrit words along with words from the regional language has been compared to setting diamonds (*mani* = Sanskrit words) with corals (*pra:vala* = regional language) that was all pervasive in literary creations of the time. This restricted the access of the majority non-Brahmin communities to existing and contemporary literature. The situation changed, as it did in other parts of India, with the coming of European Christian missionaries.

The Impact of Missionaries on transformation of Tamil Language and Literature

The first and foremost change brought about by the proselytising efforts of the missionaries was the liberation of Tamil from the clutches of high flown Sanskritised vocabulary and thus indirectly restrict the dominance of the Sanskrit knowing Brahmins. To propagate the Gospel, the Christian missionaries from the European countries used the colloquial language of the region. Like William Carey in Bengal, who studied both Bangla and Sanskrit to master the language of the common man and understand the culture of the region where he would be working, Father Henry Henriques is considersd the first European Tamil scholar of the sixteenth century.

The missionaries mingled and followed the life style of the local people. Meenakshisundaram, in his dissertation *'Contribution of European scholars to Tamil'.* (1974) refers to Robert-de-Nobili who proclaimed himself to be a 'Roman Brahmin'. He adapted to the life of the people, adopted 'harmless (Hindu) customs and ceremonies for Christian use' and studied both vernacular and Sanskrit 'with a view to achieving fluency of speech and writing and accurate knowledge of the literature of the people.' There were others like him and there is no doubt about their contribution to Tamil language and linguistics.

First and foremost, the translation of the Bible and other biblical works in colloquial Tamil promoted the development of the vernacular language. Their second major contribution was the development of the Tamil prose form. Hitherto, the verse form was predominant. The prose form was restricted to commentaries on original poetic pieces, inscriptions and official decrees.

Henceforth, both the verse and the prose forms were accepted in Tamil literature and pioneers like Nobili and Beschi used both the forms for religious and creative purposes. The missionaries were also responsible for introducing Tamil literature to the outside world. They not only translated gems from classical Tamil literature in other languages but also enriched Tamil with their creative writings. Short stories, articles, travelogues and writing of diaries introduced new genres to then existing Tamil literature. They were also responsible for bringing out books on science, medicine and other informative subjects.

The European missionaries also compiled monolingual, bilingual or even trilingual dictionaries to facilitate language learning (here colloquial Tamil) for preaching Christianity to the masses. Such intellectual endeavours, though motivated by concerns which were prompted more by missionary work than altruism, provided the necessary impetus for development of Tamil dictionaries in alphabetical order, sometimes with graphic ones for retrieval of meaning, as reference material by the common people.

Equally important was the writing of Tamil pedagogical grammar with specific purpose of language learning by the missionaries to be fluent in the language of the majority of the population. It was not the first Tamil grammar to be written, though. An ancient independent grammar, *Tolkappiyam* can be dated back to third century BC to third century AD. Such evidence of systematically written grammar is absent from other languages of the same family. However, there is no doubt that the missionaries contributed immensely to the field of descriptive and comparative grammars. 'With regard to the grammar written by

Europeans in Tamil i.e. *tonnu:l vilakham'* Shanmugam (1994) stated, 'It has shown many new insights in the organisation of phonology and grammar. Really it is nearer to the modern descriptive linguistics than to the native Tamil grammar. In more than one way, it has anticipated the birth of the descriptive linguistics in this century.' (Shanmugam, 1994). It was Robert Caldwell whose *Comparative Grammar of the Pro-Dravidian or South Indian Family of Languages* was the precursor of comparative grammar in India. His assertion that the South Indian languages did not have any 'genetic relationship with Sanskrit' was in total contradiction to the prevailing belief of both the Indian and the European scholars of that period. The genesis of the Tamil Purist movement, which we will come back to in a later section, may be attributed to this path breaking discovery.

The missionaries introduced the printing press in India. Conjunct consonants, specially geminated consonants followed by vowels were earlier written as one letter. The European practice of writing each letter separately along with the coming of the printing press transformed the Tamil graphic system. Among other modifications mention must be made of giving space between words. Earlier, Tamil words had no space when written. As the missionaries found it difficult to understand several words joined together, they started giving space between words for easy comprehension. They also introduced punctuation marks in written Tamil texts. Also, because of their interest in comparative research work, they had to refer to several authors. Such citations necessitated referring to the author along with their texts. Hence, another important change brought about by these missionaries was to practice of assigning authorship to any original work. This was totally new to the Tamil writers. The original authorship was always debatable so far but the European practice of mentioning an author along with his/her work for purposes of references introduced a happy change. According to Tamil scholars like E. Annamalai these innovations greatly simplified the task of reading with speed and comprehension.

Thus, the style followed by Europeans in prose writing is totally different from the earlier styles. Since their aim was to propagate Christianity, they adopted a style close to the colloquial Tamil. The verse style was the symbol of high caste and educated people at that time. Introduction of prose style and propagation of education among the downtrodden shattered the Symbolic function of the nexus between education and poetic form.

Impact of Globalisation and Modernisation of Tamil

The impact of the European missionaries on the development of Tamil language and literature was profound. Another off-shoot of the contact with Europeans, seventeenth century onward, was the modernisation of traditional Indian society and consequently Indian languages. Sociologists have pointed out that '...traditional societies are organised on the ideologies of societies based on religion, mythology and individuals with unequal rights.' On the other hand, the ideology of European society is organised on principles of equality, freedom of individuals and the advancement of society through knowledge based on reason. Factors like modern forms of education and industrialisation transformed traditional Indian society beyond recognition. The perception of people, beliefs and values that emerged as a result of modern education, information revolution, free trade explosion, globalisation shaped a society that was opposed to traditional ideologies.

The language that is used in different domains in a modern society requires 'new vocabulary for new areas of knowledge, new styles and registers.' (Ferguson:1962) Conscious efforts to simplify language in the areas of script, *sandhi* and syntax often mark the modernisation of language evolution.

The *Tani-T-Tamil* or Pure Tamil Movement

Robert Caldwell's epoch-making work, *Comparative Grammar of the Dravidian or both Indian Family of Languages* ushered in an era of political and social awakening in that region. This assertion that Tamil did not belong to Sanskrit or the Indo-European group of languages which is believed to be the origin of several languages prevalent even today in north India, enthused Tamil scholars.

The Tamil Purist movement began, formally, with Maraimalai Adigal in 1916. However, this attitude of using words only with Tamil roots had existed since the period of *Tolkapiyyam,* the earliest Tamil grammarian, much before the use of Sanskrit words in Tamil literature. This practice of using high-flown Sanskritised Tamil words in literary and other scholarly writings was prolonged by the privileged and elite Brahmin class to obfuscate the common people and guard their own interests and social supremacy.

Adigal began by weeding out all Sanskrit words used by him in his earlier works. He replaced them with Tamil words found in ancient inscriptions or literary sources. But Adigal soon realised that purging of all (loan) words from Sanskrit or foreign languages like English was next to impossible because of industrialisation, technological advancement, widespread use of information technology and subsequent globalisation. Post-Independence, English was not just the link language for communication all over India, but also higher education, particularly in technical and professional education. It was the language of the administration, and judiciary of free India. It became easy for English educated Indians to study abroad and look for employment in places other than their own state and own country. Hence, the 'pure Tamil' movement (before and after 1916) was mostly directed against Sanskrit, a language accessible to only a privileged few. But the utility of English in the present times was accepted by one and all and hence the purists turned a blind eye to this internationally influentially language. However, in the mid-1960s, anti-Hindi agitation gripped the state of Tamil Nadu. Self-immolation by men and women of the state of Tamil Nadu forced the Central Government to permit a two language formula in Tamil Nadu and neighbouring Pondicherry, Sumathi Ramaswamy (1998) cites different instances of self immolation as evidence of '*tamilparru*'. The scholar suggests that the lexical item '*parru*' be glossed as devotion and hence the term '*tamilparru*' be translated as Tamil devotion.

The Pedagogical Dilemma of Multilingualism in the Union Territory of Puducherry

The non-contiguous nature of the Union Territory of Puducherry has created a unique situation. As the three different constituents of the Union Territory are geographically scattered in three different states of India, there is no uniformity in the educational policy implemented in the different areas. Consequently, Yanam and Mahe follow a three language formula as have been implemented in the states of Andhra

Pradesh and Kerala, while urban Pondicherry and the rest of Puducherry on the east coast follow a two language formula like neighbouring Tamil Nadu. So different language policies are in effect in the same Union Territory.

In this section, we shall look at the ground realities that exist in Puducherry proper with reference to the status enjoyed by Tamil.

Tamil is the language of the majority of the population and because of the two language policy that is prescribed in Puducherry, students enjoy an advantage, i.e. studying two languages instead of three as is normally followed in other states of India. To obviate the existing inequality, the Government of Puducherry issued an order in 2003, that required non-Tamil as well as Tamil students who had opted for other languages, to study Tamil from classes 1 to 8. To facilitate learning of Tamil, the Government of Puducherry developed and introduced *Arimukat* Tamil for classes I to VIII. But the order is no longer implemented. We need to mention here that school students are allowed to choose either Tamil or French or Hindi as the first language. The students are also allowed to opt out of the language, they had once selected, at secondary or senior secondary level. Students who prefer Hindi or French as their first language can complete schooling without studying Tamil as the second language which in most cases happen to be English. The situation becomes more complicated in view of the fact that English medium or French medium schools do not offer Tamil as a subject. Rather, the use of Tamil is discouraged in such schools.

The multilingual character of urban Pondicherry also encourage the study of Hindi in lieu of Tamil. This is particularly observed in cases of those who belong to Yanam or Mahe as no school offers Telegu or Malayalam and the parents prefer Hindi as the first language for their children. Moreover, the presence of a bilingual Hindi speaking population and children of Central Government employees encourage the study of Hindi. The devotion to Tamil attitude as witnessed in Tamil Nadu earlier no longer prevails. Rather as the present day generation recognises and accepts the importance of English in this era of globalisation, a knowledge of Hindi has become a pre-requisite for jobs available in north India. Also the perception of the common people that Hindi and French are easy to learn and guarantee high scores in examinations in a country where scoring high marks is very important. Moreover, learning Tamil as a language is taken for granted because of the exposure in the family and the neighbourhood.

Contemporary Pure Tamil Movement in Puducherry

As a consequence of interplay of complex social, political and economic factors, the Tamil population of Puducherry has, more or less, accepted the intertwining of loan words from various sources for effective communication. The intensity of the earlier movement is much less these days. It has become more or less organisation specific, the activities of which are 'confined .... to organising literary meets and occasional public demonstration.' Nevertheless, contemporary purists are much against the use of English by Tamils. Their slogans like 'We will avoid using English' or 'We will promote Tamil which is precious' underscore their ideology. Notices criticising the use of English, attempt to raise the consciousness of Tamil people against code-mixing and code-switching—their slogans bear testimony to their ideology.

Organisations like *tanitamil iyakkam* encourage people to use Tamil names for their children. Boards with suggested Tamil names, are prominently displayed in different parts of the city. They seek to introduce new Tamil words for oft-used loan words like bun or coffee. Among their other agenda, mention may be made to their endeavour to convince the government to use Tamil for education and administration. Among their demands to the government is the one requiring officials to put their signature in Tamil. An order, to this effect, has already been issued by the government.

To meet the requirement of modern science and technology, about 3000 words have been created by the purists. Some scholars like Thomas have recommended the use of *Calque* or loan translation as a 'healthy compromise between linguistic chauvinism on the one hand and the unnecessary use of foreign words on the other.'

We can thus conclude by saying that the original Pure Tamil Movement sought to establish the vitality and independence of Tamil. The process of purification was directed against Sanskrit, the reasons for which were socio-political (i.e. undermining or destroying the dominance of Brahmins) and not just linguistic jingoism. Nowadays pure Tamil is advocated for the unification of Tamils all over the world and to develop Tamil to suit the electronic age by overcoming English. In this context, their contribution in the field of vocabulary by reviving earlier literary words is commendable. We must also remember the contribution of the European missionaries in the evolution of the Tamil language. They were path breakers and took Tamil to great heights.

Diary Tradition

Anandaranga Pillai and his diaries

Anandaranga Pillai was born in the year 1709 in Chennai. His father was a merchant. When he was twelve years old, his father moved to Pondicherry. He was earlier called as 'Anandarangappan'. He was addressed by the governors and councillors as 'Rangappa' and 'Rangappillai'.

Anandaranga Pillai was well versed in English and French. He seemed to be good in Telugu and Malayalam also as we understand from some of his corrrespondence in these languages. He started his career as a merchant with the responsibility of taking care of the textile factory at Porto Novo (now Parangipettai) in Tamil Nadu. Later he moved up as *dalal* (broker) and then as the *dubashi* (translator).

Anandaranga Pillai started writing his diary from 9 September, 1736. He continued it for twenty-five years till almost to the last days of his life. He died in the year 1761. He mentioned that he had recorded what he had heard and seen on the arrival and departure of ships. Additionally, he comment on the wonders that happened everyday.The information on the French ministry and the governors who ruled Puducherry and their activities too have been recorded.

It was Gallies Montburn who unearthed the diaries of Anandaranga Pillai. The then Governor of Chennai, Wenlock ordered the copying of the diaries to preserve and make the happening related to the British Government. While doing this, it was realised that some of the portions are missing and efforts were made to search them. Anandaranga Pillai mentioned days and dates according to both the Tamil and French calendars. He also considered putting the time—both of Europe as well as India—as he wrote the everyday happenings.

The Art and Culture department of the Puducherry Government has published the diaries of Anandaranga Pillai in twelve volumes with volume eight having two parts in Tamil. A sample page from one of Anandaranga Pillai's diaries has been produced on page 21.

(Source: Anandaranga Pillai Naatkurippu Vol 8 Part-1 Published by Art and Culture Department, Government of Puducherry in 1988)

Rangappa Thiruvenkatam Pillai and his diaries

Rangappa Thiruvenkatam Pillai, the younger brother of Anandaranga Pillai, was born in 1737. He was called 'Appaavu'. He was well versed in French and was said to be good in horoscope reading. He got appointed in 1764 by the French authorities as. In 1776 he headed the Indians on the order of French government and served as the agent for commerce. The French Governor Dupleix, appointed Thiruvenkatam Pillai as a translator when he attacked Chennai. Pillai was sent to Chennai in 1746 to compile the day to day events. The diaries written by Thiruvenkatam Pillai are available in the National Library at Paris. A few are available in Tamil Nadu Archives and in Pondicherry Archives. They cover the events that happened under and related to French rule from 1761 to 1781.

The writings in the diaries are related to the events in the family in Pondicherry. There is information on political events also. Information on the Danish company, Dutch company and French companies has been recorded. In addition, comments on the army, socio-cultural events and common events have been written by him. The diaries of Thiruvenkatam Pillai help us to understand Indian history, particularly the history of Puducherry. He died in the year 1791.

A sample page from the Diary of Rangappa Thiruvenkatam Pillai is given below.

52 ரங்கப்ப திருவேங்கடம் பிள்ளை நாட்குறிப்பு

அடைவீர்களென்னறும், இன்னும் கொஞ்ச ஞானமிலே, இதுகளெல்லாம் விசிதமாய் தெரியத்தக்கதாக யெழுதி யனுப்பிவிக்கிறோம். ஞங்கள் விலிடத்திலே சகல பிலத்துடனே சந்தோஷத்துடனே யிச்சேகக் கொண்டிருக்குறோம். சத்துருவான இங்கிலிசுக்காறர் கப்பல் மிலிடத்திலே காணத்தக்கதாக யிருந்தபடி. பிருஞ்சிலே யெழுதியிருந்ததை தமிழ்ப் படுத்தினது.

ஸ்ரீ ரும செயம்

விஷ ௵ மாசி மீ௳ உ ௬ புத்வாரம்: சதளஎசாயஉ ஆண்டு, பிவறேறு மீ௳ ய ௬

முன் யெழுதுனபடிக்கு காகிதத்துக்கு அதுவரைக்கும் மோரிசுலே யிருந்தது. நம்ம கொமுசலியேர் பிருஞ்சுகாறருக்கு இஸ்காதர் யினிமேலே யிருக்குற கப்பல் சொன்னார்கள்.

கப்பல் பெரும் பீரங்கி வயணம்

கப்பல்	பீரங்கி	கப்பல்	பீரங்கி
பிறவு	அய	லத்தீவு	சாயச
தொப்பென்றெவாம்	எயச	லீவுறித்துரு	சாயச
வலியாம்	எயச	லசீல்	சாயச
யேதுவார்	எயச	துத்தீல்	சாயச
பொருதுனெ	எயச	வறுலீக்கு	சாயச
சோதியாகது	அயச	லெபெடுந்தேன்	சாயச
பியிஞெத்தொா	எயச	தெளியீது	சாயச
கொந்துமிரவான்க	எயச	சன்லுயி	சாய
சந்தோர்	எயச	லூக்கிதொரஸியாம்	சாய
றெஞெமே	சாயச	லூக்கிபிறகொஞ்ஞிய	சாய
வாளுரைசோரம்	சாயச		
ஆக கப்பல் யக		ஆக கப்பல் ய	

கப்பல்	பீரங்கி		
தூக்கி துறுஷாம்ஷோம்	சாய	இதல்லாமல் பிறகாத்து .. ச	
லெ லீசு	சாய		
லெ கோந்தே	ருயச	ஆக உறுப்படி .. நய	
லெ பெனி	ருயச		
லெ மசீவு	ருயச		
ஆக கப்பல் ரு			

(Source: Rangappa Thiruvenkatam Pillai Diary, Vol-1, compiled by S. Jayaseela Stephen. The diary was published by *Puduvai Mozhiiyal Panpattu Niruvanam* (Puducherry Institute of Linguistics and Culture), Puducherry in 2000 in two volumes)

BHARATHIDASAN

Bharathidasan, popularly known as *Paaveendar* (king of poets) was born in 1891. His original name was Subburathinam. He resuscitated the art of Tamil poetry in the twentieth century. He was the one who strove hard to refine and modernise the Tamil language that had remained dormant for long. He was a gifted child who at the age of eleven composed poems. He underwent formal education in Tamil literature, Tamil grammar and Saiva Siddhanta Vedanta under reputed scholars. He also studied at the College Calve in Pondichery. In 1909, he was introduced to Subramanya Bharathi (Bharathiyar), and his interactions with this great poet had a great impact on him. He initially worked as a Tamil teacher in the French territory of Karaikal. Bharathidasan's contact with Bharathiyar helped him to attach himself with the multifaceted freedom movement in Tamil Nadu and Pondicherry. One of his poems has been recognised as the invocation song by the Government of Puducherry. Bharathidasan wrote under different pseudonyms. He actively participated in the Indian Independence movement through his writings. As an admirer of Gandhiji, he promoted the sale of khadi and wrote many patriotic songs. He openly opposed the British and the French Governments. He was arrested and sentenced by the French Government for fifty months of imprisonment as he voiced views against the French Government that was then ruling Pondicherry.

Bharathidasan's creations and writings comprise different genres. His love for the Tamil language and Tamil society was overwhelming. His poetic subjects vary from love, nature, women to political, social and economic problems. Apart from poems he has written essays, letters, short stories, dramas, scripts for movies, autobiography and also on linguistics. His literary writings have as their core the thoughts on different movements like the Indian National Freedom Movement, Dravidian Movement and Tamil National Movement. He was a strong supporter of Periyar and an important member of the Suyamariyadhai Iyyakam (meaning self-respect movement) and Dravida Movement, founded by Periyar. He became the voice of the Dravidian movement. Bharathidasan was conferred the title of *Puratchi Kavingyar* revolutionary poet by Periyar. He won the Golden Parrot Prize in 1946 for his play *Amaithi-Oomai* (Peace and Dumbness). He was given the Sahitya Akademi Award posthumously in 1970 for his play *Pisiranthaiyar.* The State Government of Tamil Nadu give the Bharathidasan Award annually to a Tamil poet. He served as the speaker of Puducherry Legislative Assembly.

Bharathidasan has secured his place in the history of Tamil literature for his command over Tamil language, for the wide range of poetic themes, stanza forms, metrical patterns, narrative technique and styles; the poetic intensity with which he expressed his vision of life, reforms, ideas he held and for his love of mankind. A state university named Bharathidasan University was established in Tiruchirappalli. On 9 October 2001, a commemorative stamp of Bharathidasan was released by the postal department in Chennai. Bharathidasan passed away in 1964. A museum has been established in his house in Puducherry and is being maintained by the Puducherry Government.

Puduvai Sivam

S. Sivapragasam (1908–1989) is popularly known as Pudhuvai Sivam. He is remembered even today for his contribution to the growth of Tamil literature and for the cultural growth of Puducherry as well. He is also admired for his poetic literature and political courage. Puduvai Sivam lived under French rule. His schooling was in *thinnai* (the raised portion in the front entrance of a house adjoining main door-way) and government schools. Proficient in Tamil and French, he was inspired by the poems of Subramania Bharathi and the revolutionary spirit of Bharathidasan. Naturally the imbibed spirit forced him to fight against French rule.He had his training under the tutelage of Bharathidasan especially in the art of poetry writing. Themes of equality, liberty and fraternity form the hallmark of his poetical works.

His first collection of poems dwelt on problems faced by weavers and he later wrote inspiring songs and poems. The journal *Puduvai Murasu* was used as a weapon against the British and French rulers. A social reformer, he was attracted by the self-respect movement of Periyar E.V. Ramasamy Naickkar (popuraly known as 'Thanthai Periyar' and later by the late Chief Minister of Tamil Nadu, Annadurai). He headed several organisations with the noble intention of giving language and speech training. Besides he started a publishing house called Gnayiru Book Publishers. In every respect he was responsible for the spread and growth of Dravida Munnetra Kazhakam (DMK) party in Puducherry. In his political career he had held the position of Deputy Mayor of Puducherry Municipality in 1968 and was elected to the Lok Sabha in 1969. The Tamil Nadu Government honoured him with the Bharathidasa Award in 1983. The Art and Culture Department of Puducherry Union Government celebrates his birthday every year in a grand manner. Puduvai Sivam passed away in 1989 at the age of eighty-two.

Vanidasan

Vanidasan was born in 1915 as Rangasamy and is fondly called Ettirajolu. He studied in a *thinnai* school and he is considered as the real disciple of poet Bharathidasan under whom he studied privately. He was a teacher and wrote many poems under the pen name 'Rami'. Like his mentor Bharathidasan, he propagated rationalism among the people. He also sang for the emancipation of women. He followed Periyar, the revolutionary leader in Tamil Nadu during his time and preached his views on untouchability, caste system and widow remarriage. He was fluent in Telugu, French and English. His poetry collection has been translated into English and Russian. He is respected as a poet of Tamil resurgence. He attached himself with the Dravidian movement and wrote many poems on the movement.

Tamiol Oli

Tamiol Oli was born in 1924 as Vijayarangam. When he was young, he was attracted by the poet Bharathi. He was an active worker of Dravida Kazhakam. He was not only the think tank of the Dravidian movement but also shone as a socialist philosopher. He has written epics, poems, children's songs, short stories and dramas. He became an active member of the Communist Party of India. He died in 1965. His poems have been collected and are yet to be published by the Puducherry Institute of Linguistics and Culture.

Subramania Bharathi

Subramania Bharathi also known as *Mahakavi* and *Bharathiar* was born on 11 December, 1882. He is respected as a poet, writer, journalist, social reformer, freedom fighter and as such is a multifaceted personality. He possessed great scholarship in Tamil poetry and textual creations.Through his words he spread the sense of freedom among people. He was a contemporary of Mahatma Gandhi, Bal Gangadhar Tilak, Sri Aurobindo, Chidambaram Pillai and U. V. Saminatha Iyer. His poems and essays focused on Tamil, Tamil welfare, Indian freedom, women's liberation, abolition of caste system etc. The king, Ettappa Nayakar of Ettayapuram in Tamil Nadu, gave him the title 'Bharathi' in appreciation of his literary scholarship. He was also well versed in English, French, Sanskrit, Hindi and Bengali. He translated from other languages into Tamil. He is recognised as a national poet. His famous collection of poems are *Kuyil Paattu* and *Kannan Paattu* and the drama *Paanchaali Sabadam.* Let us sing 'Vande mataram and worship our mother land' is still one of the famous lines from his poem. He was adept in composing poems in dialogue form known as *vasana kavitai* in Tamil. He worked as an editor in the daily *Sudasamitran*. He also served for the weekly *India*, *Puducherry* and a women's magazine called *Chakkravardni*. Bharathiyar passed away on 11 September, 1921.

The house where Bharathiyar lived in his birth place Ettayapuram as well as the house in which he spent his days in Triplicane in Madras have been declared as national memorials. In addition, the Government of Puducherry has converted the house where Bharathiyar lived as a museum. The Tamil Nadu Government on its part has instituted a university in Coimbatore named after the great national poet as Bharathiyar University.

In the history of Puducherry, Subramania Bharathi also has a role. Fearing arrest by the British Government for his tirade against them and movement for the freedom of India, he escaped to Pondicherry. From there he wrote many poems with the themes of national freedom, freedom for women, children's songs and devotional.

References

Meenakshisundaram, K. (1974). 'Contribution of European scholars to Tamil'. *TamilDepartment Series No. 33*. Madras: University of Madras.

Ramaswamy, Sumathi. (1998). *Passions of the Tongue: Language Devotion in Tamil India, 1891–1970*. Oakland, CA: University of California Press.

Shanmugam. 1994. 'Christians and Tamils'. In S. I. Innasi and V. Jeyadevan (eds). *Christian Contribution to Indian Language and Literature*. Madras.

3 Telugu

Introduction

Yanam, one of the four regions of Union Territory of Puducherry, is situated on the east coast of the Indian peninsula and is bound on all sides by the East Godavari district of the State of Andhra Pradesh. The Godavari river is on the northern and eastern sides of Yanam and the Koringa river is on the South.

In spite of its small size, Yanam has a historical background that dates back to 1723, when the Compagnie Française des Indes Orientales (French East India Company) established a trading post, thus making Yanam the third French Colony in India. From Colonel A. Bigot's *The Botanic Garden of Yanam*, we come to know that just after four years of setting up the trading post, the French vacated Yanam in 1727 because of slackened business, but returned again in 1731, when Haji Hassan Khan authorised Fouquet—a French representative—to set up a 'loge' (small business concession) in Yanam. In 1735, Nawab Roustoum Khan granted a *parwana* (permission or warrant) to the French for carrying out trade and commerce in the region. The French re-established themselves completely in 1742, following a *farman* (grant or permit) issued by the Mughal Emperor Muhammad Shah confirming all the concessions made to the French by Salabath Jung, the then Subedar of Deccan. History says that Bussy, the then French general had helped Salabath Jung to become the Subedar of Deccan, who not only gifted the region of Yanam to the former as a token of gratitude, but also granted many concessions in the form of *inaam* (gift or donations). This was later changed to Yanam (Yanaon in French). Later, in 1750, the sovereignty of the France over Yanam was confirmed by Muzaffar Jung, the Nizam of Hyderabad, and it continued till 1758, when the French lost Yanam to the British after a battle. There had been wars between the British and the French over Yanam and it was the British winning thrice to keep Yanam under their control. Finally, in 1817, Yanam was returned to the French following negotiations.

Yanam covers an area of 30 square kilometre and according to the 2011 Census has a population of 55,626, out of which the male population is 27,301 and remaining 28, 325 is the female population. With a literacy rate of 79.47%, Yanam is no doubt a highly developed district. Apart from Telugu being the dominant language spoken (and also the official language) in Yanam, we can also find other languages such as Tamil, Malayalam, French, and English being spoken here.

Ranga Kavi's *Anandarangarat Chandamu* written in Telugu and also *Athireyapprayap Pramanam* are significant literary pieces. Some references have been found in the historical diary of Anandaranga Pillai who served as a translator under the French Governor Dupleix. Yakshganam and Kuchipudi are the famous performing arts in this region. The festivals celebrated are Yuhati, Chitra Poonam and Sankranti.

Yanam, being the French Colony for nearly two centuries, has developed a culture that is an amalgamation of French and Telugu cultures. And it is due to this unique culture that the Telugu people from Yanam can be easily distinguished from the other Telugu immigrants. Also, Yanam Telugu as a language is slightly different from the Telugu spoken in the states of Andhra Pradesh and the newly formed state of Telangana.

Like any other region of the present Puducherry Union Territory, Yanam also rose against French domination. The Socialist Party led by Kami Setti Parasurama Naidu and the Mahajana Party headed by Yerra Jaganatha Rao and Meddime Chetty Sathya demanded this region to be merged with the Indian Union. Kami Setti Venugopala Rao Naidu started the movement to liberate Yanam and this gained momentum after R. Dadala became the Secretary of the French India Merger Congress. On 13 June, 1954 with great efforts and sacrifice by the leaders like Dadala, M. Satyanandam, Mayor of Yanam and T. Tatayya, Yanam was liberated from French rule. R.Dadala became the administrator for the time being. One representative from this region is sent to the Legislative Assembly. At present this tiny region is highly developed in all aspects.

State of Language Use

The percentage analysis of Telugu language use in Yanam shows that among the older generation, there is 12% language shift in the Naidu community and 30% shift in the Arundadiyar communities. Among the younger generation, the highest percentage of language use is 83.3% in Reddiyar and Chettiyar communities. Here also the younger generation in Naidu and Arundadiyar communities show low percentage of language use. In total, we can calculate the percentage of language shift in various communities by observing the differences in the language use patterns of older and younger generations. The percentage of language shift is 16.66% in Reddiyar and Chettiyar communites, 25% in Brahmin community, 48.88% in Naidu community and 32.5% in Arundadiyar community. Language maintenance is high in Reddiyar, Chettiyar and Brahmin communities.

The proficiency of the informant is also very helpful to measure the percentage of language shift or loss among communities. The older generation is highly proficient among the Reddiyar, Chettiyar and Brahmin communities whereas among the Arundadiyar it is 90% and in Naidu 77.77%. This is the proficiency as reported by the informants. The difference of proficiency between older and younger generations is very much significant. It is noticed that the difference in the proficiency of younger and older generations is 16.7%, 12.5%, 8.4% in the Reddiyar, Brahmin and Chettiyar communities respectively. But in Naidu and Arundadiyar communities, it is 36.33% and 28.5% respectively. It is thus clear that Chettiyar, Brahmin and Reddiyar communities take more care to maintain Telugu than the Arundadiyar and Naidu communities. This section tries to explain the reasons for language shift among the selected communities.

Domains of Language Use

As seen earlier, a domain can be seen as the configuration of at least three component factors—

- The participants in a conversation
- The place where it occurs
- The subject under discussion

In order to determine language maintenance or loss, we have to consider the habitual language use patterns in various domains.

Telugu is used only in very limited domains. There is a clear language loss in the domains of education, government, transaction, friendship etc. It is maintained in the family domain alone. In the family domain also, the language use pattern has changed considerably in the younger generation when we compare the patterns with older generation. In the Tamil-Telugu situation, there is both perceptible language shift and language loss.

Defining Power Status of Telugu Communities

Linguists define minority in terms of numerical strength only. But there are cases where the minority people dominate the majority in many socio-political activities. The criterion of numerical strength along with geographical distribution is inadequate and does not show the functional role of minority languages in a society. Hence rejecting the statistical definition of minority, Srivastava (1984) defines it by taking two variables simultaneously: one related to quantum dimensions and the other to power dimensions. The notion of language power has been characterised in terms of the following three factors:

- The wider action radius and range of usage in certain domain
- Greater degree of control over the speakers of other language
- Higher status and prestige in the eye of the people

The notion of power can be defined in many ways. For instance, Mackey (1973) has discussed six indicators of language power, namely. demography, displacement, mobility, wealth, ideology and culture. The other possible indicators could be literacy, urbanisation, educational level, population, homogeneity and political mobilisation.

Srivastava has correlated the two variables, power and quantum, as follows:

A+ +	B+ –
C– +	D– –

A – Both strength and power – High status group

B – Strength without power – Low status group

C – Power without strength – Lower group

D – No power No strength – Minority group

Generally, minority people lack power and strength when compared to majority people. If a section of minority people has power, then they can be considered as an elite group. The variation in the maintenance or loss of Telugu in the selected five communities can be explained in terms of the power status of each group. Power status is not a single concept. The indicators of power are many. For the present study, the caste status, economic and political status of the communities are taken to describe the power status.

Caste status

Most of the studies on language maintenance or loss enumerate a few factors which are responsible for the maintenance or loss of a particular case. Many western theories on language maintenance or loss do not see the Indian situation in its proper perspective. Indian society needs a separate model. This is because of the nature and type of multilingualism, minorities and their characters which are different from other societies.

In Indian society, caste and occupation are the two important variables that play a significant role in language maintenance/loss. Caste and occupation go together in traditional Indian society.

Traditional Indian society is stratified on the basis of occupations like priest, warrior-king, business people and others. Each caste is associated with status according to their occupations. Even in modern society, caste has been given importance in many spheres of social activity. It is thus an inseparable phenomenon of Indian society. From the Vedic to the modern period, caste has been nourished in the minds of the people in one form or other. It is obvious that Brahmin and Arundadiyar communities are in two extremes in high and low social status. The other communities, namely, Chettiyar, Reddiyar, Naidu are given intermediate status. Chettiyar, being a business community, comes next to the Brahmin in the status scale. The order of caste status is Brahmin, Chettiyar, Reddiyar, Naidu and Arundadiyar.

Economic status

The economic status of a community is an important factor in deciding the power of that community. Even if a community is a small one and yet if it controls the agricultural, business and other economic institutions of a place, then the community automatically acquires power of that place. This can be noticed in many Indian villages where the rural economy has been completely controlled by the minority community, which in turn places the community in the highest rung of power hierarchy of that village. In Puducherry, the Reddiyar community is very much associated with agricultural profession and the Chettiyar community with the business profession, with marginal overlapping.

There are other Tamil speaking communities like the Mudaliyar and Udaiyar who are also engaged in agricultural activities. But the Puducherry Reddiyars' share in the agriculture economy is substantial when compared with other communities.

The Rediyars also run hotels, restaurants and other important businesses. Similarly, the Chettiyars are engaged in almost all kinds of business. These two communities are economically dominant among the Telugu minority group. People from other communities are mostly employed in government services and a few are in business. Arundadiyar people are economically low in status. They practice their traditional occupation of leather works.

Political status

Political status implies the increasing participation of a particular community in the political activity of the union territory. As for the political status of language, Telugu has been recognised as one of the state languages of the Government of Puducherry. Regarding the political status of the communities, each community has a considerable population and members are elected for the legislative assembly from these communities in every election. It is a well known fact that the economically stronger communities have easy access to politics. In Puducherry, Chettiyar and Reddiyar communities are economically stronger than other minorities. But the Chettiyars are more devoted to their business than to politics. The Reddiyar community is politically more influential than other Telugu communities in this state.

As we have seen, economic and political status are interrelated. The caste status also plays a crucial role in deciding the power structure of a group. In the traditional classification, Reddiyar and Naidu communities come under Kshatriya category which is second in the order of traditional status. Arundadiyar comes under untouchables which is the lowest status in the hierarchy.

The power status of the selected communities using the three factors, caste, economy and politics are tabulated below.

Caste	Caste Status	Economic Status	Political Status
Arundadiyar	IV	V	-
Brahmin	I	IV	-
Chettiyar	II	II	-
Naidu	III	III	-
Reddiyar	III	I	+

The power status is an important parameter to measure the language maintenance/ language loss (LM/LS) of a particular community. The report on language maintenance among three small communities in Kerala notes that LM is high among high caste and low caste people. He has considered the traditional caste status only. But in an urban setting, many factors should be kept in mind while deciding the power of a particular community. Taking such factors as caste, economy and politics, the power of the selected communities can be interpreted as follows using Srivastava's classification.

- Reddiyar–power group
- Brahmin, Chettiyar–elite group
- Naidu–powerless group
- Arundadiyar–powerless group

From the survey results, it is observed that LM is high among the people of the Reddiyar community. We can attribute the power status as one of the factors for LM to an appreciable extent. Then comes the elite groups in this regard. The LM is low in Naidu and Arundadiyar communities because they command less power. When we compare the the Naidu and Arundadiyar, LM is higher among Arundadiyar than the Naidu group.

Here the caste hierarchy plays its role in Arundadiyar group. The low caste people also maintain their language like the elite and power groups.

Actual factors for language maintenance/language loss (LM/LS)

Apart from the power factor, there are several other factors which promote or hinder the language maintenance process. The factors can be classified into convergent factors and divergent factors. Convergent factors tend to unite Telugu speakers with the majority group and at the intra-language level, they unite Telugu speakers and help to maintain their language. Divergent factors are those factors that foster separation between groups.

Inter-language Convergent Factors

At the inter-language level, there are some factors which unite the Telugu speakers with Tamils. The factors listed below cause Telugu speaking community to mingle with Tamil people.

- Absence of Telugu as a medium of instruction
- Status denial or absence of land of origin contacts
- Absence of major threat
- Government policy

Medium of instruction in the mother tongue not only helps children to learn faster but also helps them to maintain their language. Absence of mother tongue education makes the students more proficient in other languages. In Puducherry, the Telugu minority people have to study Tamil since Telugu is not a medium of instruction in the Union Territory. Telugu is not at all useful for the speakers in the following sectors: (1) Job opportunities and (2) Social integration. They have to adopt the language of the majority for these purposes.

Status denial is another important factor in the Indian minority language situation. The settled Telugu minorities have no contact with their land of origin. The land of origin alienated these settled minorities as Arava Telugus. The denial of status in the land of origin makes the minorities assimilate totally with the majority. Telugus in Puducherry region do not opt for matrimonial contacts with Telugus from the land of origin. Further, the minority Telugus are rooted firmly in their new found domicile and their interests are well protected.

Inter-language Divergent Factors

The majority–minority conflict which is a major inter-language divergent factor may arise if any of the following factors is present in a given bilingual situation.

- Competition with majority people in employment, business etc.
- Oppression of minority people
- Cultural separateness
- Claim for autonomy

As far as the situation in Puducherry is concerned, it is a region of composite cultures. It is a typical multilingual, multiethnic and multicultural territory. Linguistic tolerance of the people of Puducherry is higher than others because of the presence of so many languages in the small territory. Even though the Tamil speaking population is the majority, no one can deny the rights of Telugu minorities in employment and others activities, since they became part of the territory.

The culture of the Telugu minorities is not a deviant one from that of Tamils. They are not inclined to indentify themselves as a separate group. Important festivals celebrated in Andhra Pradesh are not at all celebrated by these minorities. Their dress, food habits, and religious practices are not deviant from those of the majority people. It is very difficult to identify a Telugu speaker unless he speaks Telugu.

Government policy is a very important factor for a linguistic minority to maintain or discard its language. In Puducherry, as in any other Indian State, the rights of the minority people are well protected through the Constitution. According to Article 29(1) of the Indian Constitution, any group with a distinct language, script or culture of its own has the right to conserve it. The right can be realised under Article 30(1), 31(1). They recognise that a minority community can best conserve its language, script or culture through educational institutions. As in education, adequate provisions have been made for the use of minority languages for official purposes also. Under Article 347, the President of India can direct, in appropriate cases, that the minority language be officially recognised for use in administration, throughout a State or any part thereof, for such purposes as he may specify. Apart from this, there are constitutional provisions for issuing important government notices, rules, regulations and the like in minority languages depending upon the concentration of the group.

Inter-language Convergent Factors

So far we have considered the general factors which affect minority language maintenance. The importance of this section is to explain the reasons for the variation in the maintenance/loss of Telugu among the selected communities.

Community solidarity

Community solidarity is an important convergent factor the main function of which is to bind an individual to a group. There are many organisational modes for a group like occupation, religion, class, sex, age, caste, language and ideology. Language maintenance can be examined in terms of whether its speakers wish to define themselves as a linguistically and culturally distinct entity. Among the five communities that have been selected, the mode through which they intend to identify themselves is very helpful to explain the language maintenance act. The responses to the question, 'whether you want to identify with your group through language or caste' will throw more light on this aspect.

The following table illustrates whether an individual prefers to identify himself with his language or caste or both.

Community	Caste	Language	Both
Arundadiyar	60.00%	26.66%	13.33%
Brahmin	38.46%	30.76%	30.76%
Chettiyar	33.12%	31.25%	15.62%
Naidu	82.14%	3.57%	14.28%
Reddiyar	73.33%	13.33%	13.33%

It is interesting to note that 82.14% of people from the Naidu community and 73.33% of the Reddiyar community have reported that they identify themselves with caste in the first instance and identify with language in the second instance. But, the Brahmin, Chettiyar and Arundadiyar communities identify themselves more through language. The percentage is 26.66%, 31.25%, and 30.76% respectively. About 15% of people from each community except Brahmins identify themselves through both, language and caste. From the response, it is clear that most of the informants prefer to identify themselves through caste. The preference is in the descending order as Naidus, Reddiyars, and Arundadiyars people prefer to identify themselves more through language. The maintenance of language in these communities is therefore high. But, the survey result shows that the maintenance is high among Reddiyar, Chettiyar and Brahmin communities. This shall be explained by the factor, symbolic significance of Telugu.

Telugu as Status or Identity Symbol

Among the Telugu minority, some consider Telugu as a symbol of their identity, while others consider it as a status symbol. We have seen that in Puducherry among Telugu communities, the Reddiyar community is considered as the power group. The language of a power group will always be considered as a superposed variety. This can be explained by referring to the diaglossic situation found in Tamil. In a diaglossic situation, among the two varieties of the same language, the high variety is considered as a superposed variety and is used for some formal social functions. The formal social functions are always connected with the power group since the common man has no access to these functions. Speaking in a high variety is considered to give status to a person.

In other words we can say, the language of the power group is always a prestigious one. Another well-known example to illustrate this phenomenon is the use of Brahmin dialect by non-Brahmin Tamil speakers before Independence. Taking into consideration the status of the Brahmin community in society, the non-Brahmins had to achieve a status in society. Common people consider the use of the Brahmin dialect as something that gives them status. So the language of the power group is always associated with a status marker. The power group always tries to retain language or some special features which are not prevalent among other groups. In the case of the Reddiyars, since they are the power group, they retain their language as a status symbol. They consider that speaking Telugu gives them prestige. This can be further proved through the attitude study of the Reddiyar community. The Telugu speaking Reddiyars in Puducherry consider Karailkal Reddiyars as belonging to lower a status group since the latter have lost Telugu completely. This attitude shows that Telugu is a status symbol for the Reddiyar community and hence the maintenance of Telugu is high among them.

As for the other communities, the Chettiyar, Brahmin and Arundadiyar consider language rather than caste as an identity symbol. They consider Telugu as an identity marker rather than a status symbol. This is because of the presence of Tamil speaking groups, in these communities. As was noted earlier, Chettiyar and Brahmins have their traditional occupations along with caste status. In these communities, there are Tamil speaking Chettiyar and Brahmin people with same caste status. Komatti Chettis of the Chettiyar community speak Telugu everywhere. But there are other Chettis of Chettiyar community whose mother tongue is not Telugu but they are also engaged in business. Same is the case with respect to Brahmin community. There are Brahmins with Tamil as their mother tongue.

With a view to keeping separate identity from their Tamil speaking counterparts, Telugu speaking Chettiyars and Brahmins consider Telugu as an identity marker. It is clear from the table that 31.25%, 30.76% and 26.66% of Chettiyar, Brahmin and Arundadiyar informants consider Telugu as an identity marker. Just to keep the identity, it is necessary for them to maintain Telugu.

Language maintenance is low in Naidu and Arundadiyar communities. But in Arundadiyar community even though their social status is low, we have noticed language shift in the community. We may attribute the symbolic function of language for this type of loss. Here also we should recognise that, there are other Tamil speaking low caste people living in Puducherry. Arundadiyar people consider other people like the Parayar as very low in social status. They do not have any marital or other types of relations with these people.

With a view to maintaining group solidarity Arunadadiyar people seek to maintain Telugu. At the same time, Telugu may reveal their identity if they speak in the presence of other high caste people. So, for the Arundadiyar people, there is an identity crisis. At one level they have to use Telugu for identity purposes while at others they have to abandon Telugu because it may reveal their caste status. In rural areas, it is quite common that people belonging to Arundadiyar community live in separate areas. Every one in that area knows their identity. So in rural areas, their problem is to keep separate identity from other low caste people. This causes them to maintain Telugu. But in urban settings like Puducherry, even though they live in separate locality, they have to mingle with all sorts of people. Here language plays a dual role, group solidarity and status mobilisation.

Group solidarity is achieved in Arundadiyar community by maintaining Telugu. Status mobilisation, identification with Tamil people belonging to high social status is achieved by not using Telugu. There is thus both loss and maintenance of Telugu among the Arundadiyar community.

As for the Naidu community, they are not so strong economically and politically. In Puducherry we have classified them as a powerless group. They have a fear complex that the other Tamil speaking people may keep them at a distance if they speak Telugu. Caste is the only symbol for their identity. So language maintenance is very low in the community.

Naming practice is an important traditional linguistic reinforcement of community solidarity. We notice that names like Ramasamy Iyer, Ramachendira Reddiyar, Gopalsamy Naidu, Dhanadapani Chettiyar etc. among older people. This is a clear linguistic evidence for group solidarity. But the situation is quite different now. Due to educational advancement, group solidarity is not expressed through names. Similarly religious affiliation can be noticed in the names of the older people. Most of the Telugu people use Vaishnavite names. But due to cultural assimilation, Saivite names are also used by all the Telugu communities. Thus at the language level also we could note a major shift in these communities.

Apart from this, there are also many other factors like cohesive living, endogamy, family structure, associations, etc. which are responsible for language maintenance/loss.

Association

Giles et al (1977) propose four factors affecting language maintenance, status factors, demographic factors, institutional support factor and cultural dissimilarity. The institutional support factor refers to the extent to which the language of a minority group is represented in the various institutions of nation, region or community. Maintenance is supported when the minority language is used in various institutions like schools, radio, newspaper, church etc.

Providing governmental or administrative services in the mother tongue can stimulate maintenance. Though Telugu is given the status of official language in the Yanam region of Puducherry State, most of the governmental activities are done through English or Tamil. The medium of communication is always through the major language.

Education is very important with respect to language maintenance. If the children's proficiency in the minority language is fostered at school, then they learn to read and write in it and this contributes to maintenance. Most of the people recognise that their speech is markedly different from the speech of their state of origin.They also recognise the dialectal variations in Telugu spoken by different Telugu communities in Puducherry region. Even though there are journals, magazines, and papers available in Telugu, these are not patronised by the Telugu people for this reason.

Broadcasting in minority language can boost the language just like publishing newspaper, journals etc. Even though Telugu is recognised as one of the official languages, Telugu programmes are not broadcast from Puducherry. The only alternative for Telugu is the language based association to provide institutional support to Puducherry Telugu people. However, there is no language based association to maintain intergroup solidarity in Puducherry. Telugu speaking communities do not have a Telugu association, to promote their language. But the associations are formed on the basis of caste. Each community has its own association. The associations of Chettiyar and Arundadiyar communities are comparatively stronger than other community associations. Community festivals, marriage alliance are arranged through the associations. It is interesting to note that the proceedings of the association are conducted through Telugu but Tamil is used for recording minutes and other correspondences.

Cohesive living

The geographical distribution of the minority groups affects language maintenance and shift considerably. As long as they live cohesively in a particular area, they have better chances of maintaining their language. This is true in the Puducherry situation also. Arundadiyar people live in Arundadinagar and Govindasalai areas in Puducherry. Similarly Chettiyars live in Vysial Street and Sattiyanagar areas. Except these two communities, other groups live in all areas. The presence or absence of non-community speakers seems to be a conditioning factor for the use of Telugu outside the home domain. So Chettiyars and Arundadiyars have a better chances of using Telugu outside their homes. In the presence of non-Telugu speakers most of the Telugu speakers do not use their mother tongue. In cohesive living they have the chance of extending the domain of Telugu usage. Maintenance of Telugu among Chettiyar and Arundadiyar communities is rated high due to cohesive living.

Endogamy

Caste is an inherited phenomenon in the Indian context. If a group loses its traditional caste affinity, then we can expect the loss of language also in that group. Endogamy is an important factor in this regard. Caste and language affinities are best maintained by endogamy. Generally intercaste marriages are rare among Telugu speakers. Intercaste marriages may weaken the bond between the people and the community. There are instances of intercaste or inter-language marriages in Naidu and Arundadiyar communities. But among the Chettiyar, Brahmin and Reddiyar communities it is very rarely found. This may be considered as a factor for the high rating of Telugu maintenance in those communities.

Family is the basic social unit of the society. The traditional joint family system has been disintegrating into nuclear families due to modernisation. This disintegration has its effects on language also. Normally a child learns its mother tongue at home. In a joint family, where people representing two generations live together, there are chances for the child to learn the language of the first generation. It is observed that children from joint families speak or at least understand Telugu unlike the children from nuclear families. The children from joint families in all communities speak fluent Telugu.

Business secret preservation

Basically language is a code employed for communication purposes. If a language has a high utility value then the chances of maintaining that language are good. In the majority environment, the minority people use their language as a code for similar purposes.

In Puducherry, almost in all communities, we could see, a handful of people engaged in business. Majority of the business people belong to the Chettiyar community. Arundadiyar people are engaged in shoe making. Shops, hotels are run by other community people. However, it is interesting to note that only a few people accept that they use Telugu for conducting business.

Role of women in language maintenance/loss (LM/LS)

Society controls the speech by providing a set of norms. Linguists have identified that there is a difference in the speech behaviour of the male and the female. This is because of the different socialisation processes for boys and girls. For example, girls are taught to be submissive to their parents, brother etc. Sometimes the gender difference in speech is associated with words and expressions which are forbidden. If women are not permitted to use certain linguistic items, then new items are likely to be used and this results in vocabulary difference between men and women. Differences in social roles for men and women and different attitudes and values of the society towards them have an impact on the speech pattern. In socio-linguistics, scholars have explored this area. Much of the work is correlational in nature involving the observation that women's speech is different from that of men and then seeking appropriate means of explaining this difference in social terms. In the Indian multilingual situation, the role of women in language maintenance or loss is equally a significant one.

In traditional society, the status of women was low. Education and equal opportunities were denied to them. The suppression of women is reflected in their language as well. Non-reciprocal use of pronouns, avoidance of the use of husband's name etc. clearly reflect the status of women in our society. In rural areas girls are still not allowed to go out of their homes after attaining puberty. These social restrictions and many other social institutions make them the preserver of minority language.

Marriage is an important event in a woman's life. This institution compels women to learn their mother tongue in the minority community. We have seen that there exists identity crisis among Brahmin, Chettiyar and Arundadiyar communities because of the presence of Tamil speaking people of their caste. Language is therefore given importance in these communities. In the attitude study also, there is a significant percentage of informants who prefer a spouse with a good command over their mother tongue.

Women transmit models to their children. Language and social norms are transmitted from one generation to the next through the process of socialisation. If a women in a family does not know Telugu, then there will be loss of language in the coming generation. The presence of elder female members in a family helps the younger people of that family to maintain Telugu. It was observed in a few cases, that both husband and wife use Tamil when they converse among themselves but they use Telugu with older female members. Here the older women act as a catalyst to preserve Telugu. In another case, a child who was brought up by his/her grandmother spoke Telugu even when the parents did not speak that language. Such phenomena are observed among Naidu and Brahmin communities.

It is also observed that the retrieval of Telugu is higher among women than men. Women pick up Telugu when they are married to a Telugu speaking family. But in the case of males, once the language is lost, they are never able to retrieve it. In such a type of situation there is total displacement of Telugu in the family.

Intra-language Divergent Factors

There are certain factors which compel the speakers of a particular community to abandon Telugu. These are:

- Testing of stigmatised features of a particular group
- Caste hierarchy
- Inter-caste marriages
- Migration from group members
- Higher education

It is noticed that the minority children feel that their Telugu is being criticised by Tamil speakers.

But within Telugu peer groups also, we have seen that each dialect has its own characteristic features. Use of these features will reveal the identity of the community to which the speakers belong to. The speakers of low caste may avoid using Telugu to conceal their identity from the other Telugu speakers. So caste hierarchy and the use of stigmatised features inhibit speakers from using Telugu.

Apart from inter-caste marriages i.e., marriage with Tamil speakers, higher education through Tamil or English medium and migration from their group have a considerable influence on the maintenance of Telugu.

So far we have seen the causal factors for the maintenance/loss of Telugu in the bilingual situation of Puducherry. We have noticed two broad categories of factor, namely, convergent and divergent, which make the speakers to associate or disassociate with Telugu speakers. These two factors are further analysed at inter-language as well as intra-language levels. We can not clearly indicate particular factors which are responsible for the loss/maintenance of Telugu in a particular community. We can identify some of those factors as explained before. The above factors have overall influence in the maintenance/loss of Telugu.

References

Giles, H., R. Y. Bourhis and D. Taylor. 1977. 'Towards a theory of language in ethnic group relations'. In H. Giles (ed.) *Language, Ethnicity and Intergroup Relations*. London: Academic Press.

Mackey, W. F. 1962 (1973). 'The description of bilingualism'. *Canadian Journal of Linguistics*, 7, 51–58.

Srivastava, R. N. 1984. 'Linguistic minorities and national languages'. In Florian Coulmas (ed.). *Linguistic Minorities and Literacy*. Berlin: De Gruyter Mouton, 99–114.

4

Malayalam

Introduction

Malayalam, sometimes referred to as Kairali, is a language spoken in India, predominantly in the state of Kerala. It is one of the twenty-two scheduled languages of India and was designated a classical language in India in 2013. Malayalam has official language status in the state of Kerala and in the Union Territories of Lakshadweep and Puducherry. Malayalam belongs to the Dravidian family of languages and is spoken by some thirty-eight million people. It is also spoken in the neighbouring states of Tamil Nadu and Karnataka, with more populace in the Nilgiris, Kanyakumari and Coimbatore districts of Tamil Nadu, and the Dakshina Kannada and Kodagu districts of Karnataka. In the Union Territory of Puducherry, the status of Malayalam needs to be seen in a perspective which is slightly different from its status in Kerala, where it has a predominant position.

In Puducherry, as has been widely known, French was the official language of French India (1673–1954), Its official language status was preserved by '*Traité de Cession*' (Treaty of Cession) signed by India and France on 28 May, 1956. It remained as de jure official language of Pondicherry by the 'Article XXVIII' of the *Traité de Cession* which states '*Le français restera langue officielle des Etablissements aussi longtemps que les répresentants élus de la population n'auront paspris une decision différente*' (the French language shall remain the official language of the Establishments so long as the elected representatives of the people shall not decide otherwise).

During the early twentieth century, Tamil had got equal status along with the existing French language but after independence in 1962, Telugu and Malayalam also got the same status but with some restrictions.

Malayalam is the predominant language in one of the districts of the Union Territory of Puducherry, namely Mahe. The Mahe sector consists of two parts: the picturesque town of Mahe, with its buildings situated on the left bank of the Mahe river close to its mouth and the isolated tract known as Naluthrara, on the right bank, comprising the four villages of Chambara, Chalakara, Palour, and Pandaquel. As one of the official languages of Puducherry at regional level, 4.8% of the population in the Union Territory of Puducherry speaks Malayalam. As of the 2001 Census, the number of people speaking Malayalam in Mahe District is 36,823.

It is also widely used in Yanam, one of the four regions of the Union territory of Puducherry, which is closer to the State of Andhra.The Malayalee population is also in considerable strength in Puducherry and Karaikal districts of Union Territory of Puducherry. However, in other districts of Puducherry except Mahe, Malayalam does not have any mentionable status. This leads to the confirmation that the status of Malayalam varies by districts in the Union Territory of Puducherry.

Malayalam is widely taught at the school level as an important subject in Mahe and children are encouraged to converse in the vernacular medium. It is taught as Part I subject in schools in Mahe. As far as the literary works in Malayalam is concerned in the Union Territory of Puducherry, there have been no such contributions available. Few writings by individuals are found which are meant only for local circulation. This has resulted in the adoption of Malayalam as one of the official languages of Puducherry and reaffirms the intense devotion and dedication of the indigenous local population to their strong roots.

The following table displays the pan-Indian presence of Malayalam, which in turn shows the pattern of outward migration of the Malayalam speaking population within India. All states and UnionTerritories of India show Malayalam speech community.

TABLE 4.1 DISTRIBUTION OF MALAYALAM SPEAKERS IN DIFFERENT STATES AND UNION TERRITORIES OF INDIA

Kerala	30,803,747	Odisa	10,440
Karnataka	701,673	Jammu and Kashmir	10,063
Tamil Nadu	557,705	Jharkhand	8,783
Maharashtra	406,358	Assam	8,141
Delhi	92,009	Arunachal Pradesh	5,583
Gujarat	67,838	Nagaland	3901
Andhra Pradesh	62,214	Uttarakhand	2,870
Lakshadweep	51,555	Bihar	2,674
Madhya Pradesh	48,515	Chandigarh	2,356
Pondicherry	42,782	Meghalaya	2000
Rajasthan	33,975	Dadra and Nagar Haveli	1,839
Andaman and Nicobar	28,869	Tripura	1,747
Chhattisgarh	26,319	Mizoram	1,322
Uttar Pradesh	19,683	Himachal Pradesh	1,231
West Bengal	17,043	Manipur	1,231
Goa	15,081	Daman and Diu	1,166
Haryana	13,989	Sikkim	1,021
Punjab	10,669		

Evolution of the name Malayalam

The general perception on the individuation of Malayalam from proto Tamil-Malayalam subscribes to a deep rooted ancestry. But it is paradoxical that the in situ origin of the name 'Malayalam' for the language is quite a recent one. The origin of the word Malayalam has long been a perplexing problem. Today, Malayalam is well recognised as the name of the principal language spoken in Kerala and Lakshadweep. It denotes an important Dravidian language.

Etymology of the words—Malayalam and Keralam

Malayalam, a major literary language of South India with long traditions of literature and scripts, is the main language of Kerala and that of Lakshadweep Islands which are 200–400 kilometre away from the south west coast of India.

Malayalam is a combination of *mala* 'mountain' with any of the following terms: *alam* 'the place denoting the mountain country' *aalam* 'depth', representing 'the land that lies between the mountain and the deep ocean' or *aal* 'man', meaning 'mountain dweller'. The last term may convey the original meaning of Malayalam denoting the people depicted by word forms such as *malayaalar*, *malayaali, malanaattukaaran* and the region or country as in the term *malanaatu.* Early variants include *malayaalma, malayaayma,* and *malayaanma*. Malayalam may be a later variant. *Lilatilakam*, a famous fourteenth century work on the grammar and language of Malayalam, mentions only *Keralabhaasa* to denote the language.

The etymology of the word *keralam* is unsure. It may have been derived from the classical Tamil word *ceralam* 'mountain slope' or *cheralam* 'land of the Cheras'. It may also have stemmed from *keral -am, kera* 'coconut tree', *alam* 'land or location' meaning 'land of the coconut trees'. Malayalis, the natives of Kerala refer to their land as Keralam. The earliest attestation to the name *kerala* is found in an Asokan rock inscription of third century BC which mentions a state or people called *kerala putra*. In literary records, *kerala* was mentioned in the Sanskrit epic *Aityreya Aranyaka*. Besides, Katyayana, Patanjali and Pliny showed familiarity with Kerala. In the last centuries BC, Kerala became famous among the Greeks and Romans for its spices, especially pepper. Regarding the origin of *keralam,* there is a legend that Lord Parasurama regained this land from the sea by standing higher on Gokarna and commanding the sea to recede, and hurling his battle axe into the Arabian Sea. The emergence of the land, thus coming out of the sea waters came to be known as Keralam.

The use of the word Malayalam, as the name of the language has not been credited with a long history. The attestation of it, in the sense of denoting a language, in the available records could be traced back only to the middle of nineteenth century. The earliest available reference to the word as '*Malayaalabhaasha*' is found in Bailey's *paLaya Niyamam* (Old Testament) published in 1839. Till date, the existing scholarship has not been able to confirm that the word *Malayaalam* was used as the name of the language earlier to this work. Earlier to nineteenth century, the available record reveals that the language of the former Kerala region was named as TamiL and then later named *Keralabhaasha* before the commencement of the current name. The prevailing understanding about the names of the language of the then region particularly *Malainaaṭṭu TamilL, Malayaayma, MalayaaLma* and *MalyaaNma* suggest the quest for independent naming of the newly shaped distinct tongue by which to declare separate identity. The word Malayalam was used earlier to refer to the region as a toponym. A clear distinction then existed between the land and the language.

Malayalam refers to the place of occupation and the words like *MalayaaLma*, or *Malayaayma* are used to mean the language. Why using the word Malayalam had not become imperative for the earlier scholars is not explicit. There are diverse etymological explanations available on the origin of the word Malayalam. The compound word Malayalam formed by combining *Malayam* (southern part of *Sahyadri* mountain) + *āḷam* – low land–lowland found in the southern part of *Sahyadri*. '*Mala*' mountain, combines either with *aḷam* 'land' to mean 'mountainous land' or with *āLam* 'depth' i. e., sea; to mean the land that lies between the mountains and the deep sea, or *mala* 'mountain' + *aal* (from the verb *āluka*–'habitation/ possession'+ *am*(suffix) 'possessor of mountain' i.e., *MalayaalaR* and their language is Malayalam. Of these, language of *MalayaalaR* is the most appealing one. The earlier referred forms *Malayaayma, MalayaaLma* and *MalyaaNma* are different forms of the same verb *āluka* – 'to possess /inhabit/ control'. But the extant records suggest that the word Malayalam initially referred to the land than to the people or language. The reason behind such an initial appearance of the term can be explained by looking at the cultural geography of the people inhabiting the region. The geographical separation by the Western Ghats, which acted as a boundary, was the initial identity of the then existing groups. It is primordial to name the area of occupation by insiders and / or by outsiders. Such label signifies the reference to self or to others. There is no separation of language and land within the primordial understanding. It is strands in continuity. Optimum resource utilisation, resource crunch, population pressure, fission etc. could mobilise people from core areas to unoccupied lands. Reduction in the face-to-face interaction makes people's language diverge and then develop into linguistically autonomous groups with cultural homogeneity (continue to remain in the former cultural ties) or heterogeneity (adapting to new cultural norms). Despite the difference in place of occupation, the ethnic and linguistic continuity prevails until the language changes. In this context, the people colonising the mountainous land from an already existing stock allow to distinguish place of occupation and language. The probable scenario was that they must have named or others referred to the land as*MalainaaDu* and the language as *Malainaaṭṭu TamiL* and the group as *Malayan / MalayanmaR(colloquiallyMalayaam/ Malayaanma–deleted plural marker*–inhabitants of the mountain).The geographical isolation, external contacts, economic autonomy later supported in sculpting new identity markers. The west coast ecology made the group to have social selection of cultural distance and then it formed a separate cultural group. As part of elite dominance, the newly emerged group must have called themselves or received the name *Mala āḷaR* (people who control the mountains). The newly emerged linguistic consciousness re-lexified *MalainaaDu* by the word *MalanaaDu* as part of the change of ai>a. Later, the country of *MalayaalaR* was named *Malayalam.* The then evolving language was christened separately as *Malayaayma, MalayaLma and MalyaaNma* as a corrupted form of *Malayaam/ Malayaanma* to mean 'native speech'. The common folk continue to get identified by Malayaam/ Malayaanma which reflects the land, people and the language. The political settings have given more popularity to the power laden *MalayaalaR* than the native *Malayaam/ Malayaanma*. The missionary sensibility tries to define the language of the people first as *Malayaam peecha* (language of the mountain people—1599— *Udayam peroor records*), *Malayaayma* (1829—*Putiya Niiyamam*–Bailey's New Testament) and later, they used–*Malayaala bhaasha* in the sense of the language of the *MalayaalaR*. It first appeared in 1839. Subsequently, Gundert used this term in 1851 and 1868. *MalayaaLma* had been in concurrent use to denote the language in 1863 (*MalayaaLmayute vyakaraNam* – 'Grammar of MalayaaLma'). The language name, Malayalam had been contributed to the literary circle by the missionary scholarship. Thereafter, land, language and people had separated and survived in an interrelated manner as *MalayalanaaDu, Malayali* and Malayalam.

Geography of the Malayalam language

Geography of language describes distribution of a language through history and space. Kerala, the present homeland of Malayalam, came into existence as a state in the Indian Union on 1 November, 1956 with a clear cut political boundary. It is a small strip of land at the southwestern part of the Indian subcontinent, extending over an area of 1.3 % of the total area of India and lying between 8° 18` and 12° 48` north latitude and 74° 52` and 77° 24` east longitude. It is bounded by the Western Ghats on the east and theArabian Sea on the west. It shares its border with the state of Karnataka in the north and the rest with Tamil Nadu. The highlands slope down from Sahyadri (Western Ghats), the midlands, area found between mountains and lowlands and the lowlands (Coastal region) define the physiographic pattern of Kerala. It was formerly a larger piece of land stretching between Kanyakumari in the south and Gokarna in the north under Chera rule. The Chera kingdom was established first in Kuṭṭanāṭu—the land lying between Quilon and Ponnani—and subsequently expanded and they were in full control of Kerala and a large part of Tamil Nadu until sixth century AD. Malayalam language geography cannot be fixed as parallel to the geography of the Chera kingdom. The genesis of Malayalam is rooted to the Chera regime but it does not confirm the language spread. Cankam Tamil was a literary language common to both Kerala and the modern Tamil Nadu from the first to third centuries AD. The common heritage coupled with political dominance allowed the *centamil* literary ancestry to continue until about AD 1600.

There are different opinions about the origin of Malayalam—whether it originated by splitting from proto-Tamil Malayalam or from middle Tamil. It ranges from fifth to ninth century AD. Inscriptional evidences confirm its official use around ninth century. Glotto chronology suggests the divergence of Tamil and Malayalam around the seventh century. From there, Malayalam language geography survives in four spaces viz. geographic, ethnic, social and diaspora across ages. The age of Kulasekharas or second Chera. It was during the reign of Rajasekhara Varman that the Malayalam Era known as Kollam Era commencing AD 825 came into existence. This political signature confirms the maturity of Malayalam identity.The period following the fall of the second Chera Empire in AD 1102, saw the rise of several independent principalities such as Venad (Travancore), Perumpatappuswarupam (Cochin), kingdoms of the Zamorin of Calicut and the Kolathiri of Chirakkal in north Kerala. Malayalam continued as principal language in these regions but distinctively maintained its regional characters. Neither the Portuguese and Dutch intrusions nor the Mysore invasion (1766–82) which disturbed the old social order—Brahmin-Kshatriya-Nair nexus—disturb Malayalam language geography. The British who helped local rulers to resist Mysore invasion later emerged as the masters of Kerala. The language geography was first disturbed by the British as they annexed Malabar under Madras presidency. In the nineteenth century, both Travancore and Cochin remained princely states. During these periods language geography was fractured. Formation of new Travancore-Cochin State after Independence made language geography more stable. This was followed by the emergence of unilingual state—Kerala—comprising the Malabar district and Kasargode Taluk of Madras state and Travancore Cochin State excluding Tamil speaking areas of south Travancore. This situation helped Malayalam language to define its boundary with the neighbouring languages—Tamil, Kannada, Tulu and Kodagu.The contact zones in south and north (Thiruvananthapuram-Kanyakumari / Kasargode/ Mangalore etc.) are managed through healthy bilingualism. Removal of Kanyakumari from the Malayalam geography disturbed the language map, but it did not create mutilated sub-regional linguistic identity due to the long survived bilingualism and adaptability of Malayalam speakers to switch over to the host tongues.

Malayalam has a second homeland in the Lakshadweep Islands, the smallest Union Territory of India. This archipelago comprises thirty-six islands and the dominant language is Malayalam. Local legends connect the colonisation of the Island to the period of Cheraman Perumal, the last Chera King of Kerala. Besides these two major regions, Malayalam extends its boundary across India and abroad and forms Malayalam speech Islands.

Linguistic geography explains the intra-linguistic regional variations. This way, Malayalam possesses regional dialectal variations in accordance to the cultural zones—North, Central and South. After the formation of the state, a unique textbook culture has been developed. Simultaneously, mass media like Akashavani, Doordarshan and print media unified Kerala which in turn helped to erase the former regional boundaries from Malayalam. Standard Malayalam neutralises this variation at communication level. Lakshadweep Malayalam is an important dialect with many archaic features of old Malayalam.Diaspora made Malayalam to survive in contact with other languages across the globe which in turn provides different geographies for Malayalam.

	2, 674
Chandigarh	2, 356
Meghalaya	2, 000
Dadra and Nagar Haveli	1, 839
Tripura	1, 747
Mizoram	1, 322
Himachal Pradesh	1, 231
Manipur	1, 231
Daman and Diu	1, 166
Sikkim	1, 021

Current status of Malayalam

Malayalam is one of the scheduled languages of India. It enjoys the shared official language status along with English in homeland Kerala and Lakshadweep. It is also counted as an official language in Puducherry. Malayalam survives as the principal mother tongue in Kerala and has 99.54 % of speakers at state level, which is the highest compared to any other state's mother tongue status in India. It survives with three major distinct regional dialects and bottom line caste dialects along with a standard form. Malayalam embraces diglossia which is neutralised due to a high literacy. As a standard language, Malayalam is rich and dynamic in its existence. About 170 daily newspapers, 235 weekly and 560 monthly periodicals are published in Malayalam. In the educational realm, it is used as a medium of instruction only at school level in the state. Its use in higher education is not encouraged at present. Decline in mother tongue education is counted as a threat to the vitality of Malayalam language in future.

Malayalam is used in mass communication both in print and electronic media. Highly appreciable visibility of Malayalam in the domain of mass communication is recorded. The survival of Malayalam as a language of diplomacy is negligible but indelible as the bottom line language in commerce locally. It has a well developed advertisement culture, by which the processing of product information is potentially ensured. Use of Malayalam in the domain of religion is somewhat secondary. Malayalam could not so far replace Sanskrit from the Hindu and Arabic from the Islamic religion, although it has replaced Syriac from the Christian faiths in the state . Its use in religious propaganda is effectively practised. Use of Malayalam is abundant in political practices. As a language of political expression, it has been well credited with a political dialect and language proficiency in this domain is well counted in bothoral and written media. Malayalam also inherently serves as a gendered language by stereotyping the feminine world. Acquired political awareness and interventions could partially influence the written language but anti-feminine outlook strongly survives in spoken Malayalam. In the domain of culture, Malayalam survives with great antiquity and prestige in the folk arts of Kerala. The role of Malayalam in classical art tradition is secondary. It is well received in films and other popular entertainments. The entertainment industry in Malayalam shows stable market trends. Although an administrative decision to use Malayalam in the judiciary was taken in 1978, the medium of judiciary has not changed to Malayalam. So is the case with the administrative use of Malayalam. As far as science and technology is concerned, Malayalam could so far survive in embracing the knowledge in popular science. Malayalam is not yet fully compatible with language technology but has succeeded in the initial phase of Malayalam computing. Its web presence has grown steadily.The state is yet to be a member of the Unicode consortium. However, the ongoing language technology initiatives suggest that Malayalam can achieve higher status in near future. As a knowledge transmission media, it has been attested with new genres of world thoughts. While it accommodates the theoretical innovations in social science and humanities with ease, its capability for displaying science and mathematics needs further terminological advancement. Its use as literary language and popular media has achieved respectable heights. The desire to accommodate knowledge into popular culture promotes the production of popular science and social science literature. Its language products like dictionaries, glossaries, grammars and other pedagogical products have to become more systematic, scientific and current in order to develop discourses in the sciences and social sciences. As translation is inequitably responding to the growing demands in various fields of knowledge, technologically compatible Malayalam with machine translation capability is the need of the hour. However, this is still in the early stages. Growth of Malayalam is represented by its cosmopolitan outlook. Accommodating elements from other languages freely to its system is its character. Modernisation of Malayalam is marked by the script and style reforms, neologisms and the standardisation processes. Free use of English words in Malayalam sentences, as freely as it did with Sanskrit in the past, is the cosmopolitan trademark of Malayalam. Malayalam also declares an existence above the parochial and provincial prejudices as a state of mind rather as a primordial confinement.

5 French

The Merger of French India

Till the Independence of India, there was no movement against the French in Pondicherry. The nationalists here worked for the liberation of India from British rule. Indian leaders advised them to do nothing adverse to the French who had been protecting Indian patriots who had taken refuge here. With a view to satisfying the wishes of the people for greater autonomy and to prepare the ground for an eventual transfer, France declared Pondicherry, Karaikal, Mahe and Yanam as free towns having complete control over individual administrative powers and placed them under the common authority of the Commissioner of the Republic in Pondicherry by a regulation dated 17 November, 1947. Chandernagore which was granted separate status on 30 June, 1947, was made a free town on 6 December, 1947. Whereas the regulation raising Chandernagore as a free town was given effect to, the regulation in respect of the other establishments was resisted by the Council of Government though it was a progressive step in the way of devolution of powers and of better governance.

Wishes of the people

Though the general assembly of the municipal councillors of Pondicherry, Karaikal, Mahe and Yanam fixed the referendum on 11 December, 1949, they were not very happy about the referendum. Their forgone conclusion was merger with India. Their sole preoccupation was the modalities of the merger. So the assembly wished to get from the French and the Indian Governments all clarifications regarding the future of French India.

It is worth noting that the French establishments had a course of history different from the rest of India. The administrative practice, the legal framework, the official language, and the medium of education were French. The elite who had French education were very anxious about their future. That they were sincere in their decision for merger was evident from the fact that they had started putting their children in English medium schools. But they wanted the merger to take place through a treaty of cession in the negotiation of which they were allowed to participate in order to safeguard the special interests of the people of Puducherry. They wanted a period of transition of twenty-five to thirty years. The assembly therefore elected a delegation of three members to contact the respective governments in Delhi and Paris to put forth the aspirations of the people and to get the assurances of those governments on the period and the modalities of transition.

Main features of the agreement

The provisions of the treaty with respect to nationality cannot be said to be satisfactory. French citizens of Pondicherry were from quite different backgrounds, ranging from an European with French as his mother tongue and an Indian hailing from a far off village who had never heard a word of French. Subjecting them to the same treatment was neither fair nor realistic. A distinction could have been made between those who had earlier opted to be governed by the French Civil Code and those who were not covered by it, as it was done thereafter in respect of other erstwhile French colonies. The failure to do so has created a separate category of Indian citizens governed by the French Civil Code as it stood in the year 1954. Modifications made thereafter by the French Parliament would not apply to them since they were no longer French. They were subject to a law which remained static and had become obsolete in many respects, which was not known well in the legal world in spite of steps taken towards amelioration. It would be better to admit those persons to the benefits of the modern Indian laws of modern India.

At the time of transfer some people had put forth the idea of dual nationality. In fact Sri Aurobindo in his message to the Nation on 15 August, 1947, at a time when nationalism was at its peak advised: '….there must grow up an international spirit and outlook, international forms and institutions must appear, perhaps such developments as dual or multilateral citizenship, willed interchange or voluntary fusion of cultures.' However, the idea was brushed aside with equal vigour by both India and France. Thereafter France reconciled herself to the idea of dual nationality and has taken steps to implement it in her territory in respect of persons having a nationality of some of her erstwhile colonies. But India is still vigorously opposed to the idea of dual nationality.

Even though dual nationality is not officially accepted, dual nationals exist in reality. As per Indian law any person born in India is an Indian citizen. As per the French Law any one born to a French national is French. So children who were born after 16 August, 1962 to French parents have got dual nationality by law. But there is no administrative mechanism to take care of such cases. So those persons can, at a time enjoy only one of their nationalities the other remaining dormant. France wants Pondicherrians to settle down in Puducherry instead of migrating to France and India wants Pondicherrians to invest in India. The government may perhaps one day take administrative measures to give full effect to existing dual citizenship situations.

Rights of French citizens

French citizens residing in Puducherry have been given special rights. As per Article 17, French nationals domiciled in the French establishments on 1 November, 1954, shall enjoy in these establishments the same freedom of residence, movement and trade as the other inhabitants of the establishments. In the agreed Proces-Verbal dated 16 March, 1963 that right was extended to those who had elected their domicile in the former establishments before 16 August, 1962. The Agreed Proces-Verbal further gives full details of all the rights which the French nationals will enjoy. Though according to the law, the rights are very extensive and confer upon permanent French residents important rights, making them in that respect almost equal to Indian citizens, there are difficulties in matter of implementation of those rights.

As far as the right of residence is concerned, if those French citizens remain confined in the establishments, there is no problem, but when they want to go to France or any other foreign country and come back, they have to get a visa of entry and for that purpose they are enjoined to have a residential permit which is renewed from time to time. In this manner they are assimilated to ordinary foreigners and are deprived of the benefit of the treaty. Right of residence implies necessarily the right to travel without any hurdle, otherwise it is illusory. The implementation of the provisions of the treaty in letter and spirit would require that French nationals domiciled in Pondicherry as on 16 August, 1962 get from the Indian Government identity cards with a right of permanent residence and travel without visa. This will also have the advantage of providing the Indian Government full data in respect of all those residents who are approximately 8,000 in number.

Regarding the economic and financial rights, though there are ample provisions in the Treaty and the Agreed Proces-Verbal they have not been incorporated in the respective Indian Acts and Rules. So the concerned Indian administrative departments are not prepared to implement them. Among these rights, one that has given room for complaints , is the right of owning immovable properties. There have been periodical notices from the Reserve Bank of India to some of the French nationals of Puducherry to show cause why they had not informed the concerned authorities about their assets. Each time the matter was closed only after the intervention of the French Consulate. The identity card referred to above, incorporating the gist of their rights would enable these nationals to get their rights as per the treaty, recognised by the Indian administration whenever required.

Cultural matters

These questions have been pre-occupying the mind of the French Government from the start and elaborate provisions to that effect were made in the agreement between France and India. The main provisions may be classified under three heads. The first one is that French language shall remain the official language as long as the elected representatives of the people shall not decide otherwise. In reality, immediately after the de facto transfer, English has acquired the place of pride. That was the language of Heads of Departments sent by New Delhi. Because of this, a switch over to English in administrative correspondence happened. Puducherry officers had to improve their skills in English in order to be of some relevance. More and more English speaking officers were recruited. After the de jure transfer, many Pondicherry officers who opted for French nationality, were incorporated in the French metropolitan cadres and left the territory. So when the Legislative Assembly of Pondicherry decided on 3 April, 1965 that English, Tamil, Malayalam and Telugu will be official languages concurrently, French had practically ceased to be in use for official transactions.

The second provision is in respect of course of studies in French. It is embodied in Article 2 of the protocol, which provides that such a course shall be maintained during the appropriate transitional period in a sufficient number of educational institutions. French medium courses were, in fact, maintained scrupulously by the Indian Government in a sufficient number of schools and the transition from the French pattern of education to the Indian one was effected smoothly, under the leadership of officers having had French education. As a sequel of this policy, there are still some Indian-run French medium schools with skeletal attendance. The standard is continuously on the decline and has reached a very low level in spite of all steps taken. It is high time that the French lycee run by the French government takes in its fold all pupils who are French nationals. In the meantime the Puducherry Government should gather in one or two institutions all pupils scattered in several schools with very poor strength in order to ensure better supervision.

The third provision is in respect of cultural cooperation. Towards that effect new institutions like the French Institute, a branch of Ecole Française d' Extreme Orient, and the Alliance Francaise have been set up soon after the transfer. Scholarship for Indians for pursuing higher training in various fields has been offered. Short time deputation of about two to four weeks of highly qualified French professors has also been resorted to. All this has produced good results on the whole. On the contrary, deputation of French teachers to Indian institutions for one year or more ended mostly in failure.

Political status

As far as Chandernagore was concerned, there was no specific provision regarding the political status of that territory in the corresponding treaty of cession dated 2 February, 1951 which came into force on 9 June, 1952. So, the Indian Parliament by Chandernagore (Merger) Act, 1954, which came into force on the 2 October, 1954, made it a part of the District of Hooghly in the State of West Bengal. However, the Government of West Bengal taking into consideration the large amount of autonomy that the Territory was enjoying, made it a Municipal Corporation, a status given only to big cities and entailing more powers than those conferred on a municipality of a town, by the Chandernagore Municipal Act, 1955.

In the treaty of cession of the other establishments which came into force on 16 August, 1962, article 2 provides that they will keep the benefit of the special administrative status which was in force prior to 1 November, 1954 and that any constitutional changes in this status which may be made subsequently shall be made after ascertaining the wishes of the people.

Before 1 November, 1954 the French establishments constituted one of the overseas territories of the French Union enjoying a sizeable amount of self-government. It was distinct from France and had a juristic personality of its own. It was even a party to some international conventions like the convention dated 24 April 1926 on the international driving permit.

After the de-jure transfer, Pondicherry was made a Union Territory of the Indian Union in 1962 by the 14th Amendment to the Constitution. The Government of Union Territories Act, 1963, along with the Rules of Business made provisions for its future governance. This change was brought about without any consultation of the people, but with the consent of the political class. If the present arrangement is compared to the one obtaining before transfer, one would find that there is lesser degree of autonomy and that the territory lost its juristic personality and financial independence. On the other side there is a more representative and more majestic apparatus of government. In order to get corresponding power, political parties have been clamouring for statehood for Puducherry.

A Vestige of the Past Or a Link-Language of the Future?

A total revolution took place in the field of education under the French rule. Education which was hitherto confined to a class of society—Brahmins and the rich was now opened to all. France, a country which held aloft the banner of liberty, equality and fraternity, could do nothing but open education to all in her colonies. Moreover, the French needed with fluency, to run the administration of the settlements. Hence, the French administrators of the Indian settlements considered education as their chief concern and opened it to all.

In Puducherry, there are many avenues for learning French or the teaching of French or the teaching in French. The main motivation here to learn French is either to score high in exams, or for better job opportunities or else to visit or work in France. Even the medical students of the local Jawaharlal Nehru Institute of Post-Graduate Medical Education and Research (better known as JIPMER) have to obtain a diploma in French before leaving the institute.

Puducherry was once the centre of the French establishments in India, and to facilitate oral and written communication with the locals and propagate the French language, the French administration had created primary and higher secondary schools where French was taught. The primary school education lasted five years and consisted of the *Cours preparatoire* (two years), *Cours elementaire* (one year), *Cours moyen* (one year) and *Cours superieur* (one year), and the medium of instruction all along was French. The exams of *Brevet Elementaire, Brevet Superieur and Certificat d'Aptitude Pedagogique* were introduced in 1885 for the higher classes. The system of *Baccalaureat de l'Enseignement Secondaire* (already instituted in 1898 at Pondicherry) was reorganised in France and the new model introduced at the school secondary level in Pondicherry in 1928. After Indian Independence, the French educational system in Pondicherry was modified and adapted to suit the national aspirations of the Indians. Subsequently, French in Pondicherry got reduced to being just a second language in the local schools. However, in the Sri Aurobindo International Centre of Education, established in 1952, students are proficient both in English and French as English is mainly the medium of instruction for English studies, history and geography, and French is the medium of instruction for French studies, mathematics and sciences.

The exclusive teaching in French as the sole medium of instruction is done primarily at the Lycee Français or the Ecoles Indiennes à Programmes Français (E.I.P.F.) like the Pensionnat de Jeunes Filles or the College Calve. However, a lack of proper finances and teaching aids seem to threaten the smooth functioning of the E.I.P.F., which now have a large percentage of drop outs; the number of admissions was around 600 in 1990, and now it is around 300. Due to many such problems, the French Section of the St. Joseph de Cluny School had to be closed, and its remaining students were absorbed by the Lycee Français, resulting in a lack of space and packed classes.

So, strictly speaking, in Puducherry, there remains only one educational institution where one can learn French from the nursery to the higher secondary and that school is the Lycee Français where French is the primary language, English is the second language and Tamil or Spanish are the third optional languages. Founded in 1826 as College Royal by the Viscount Desbassyns de Richemont, it was first meant only for Europeans. Then, in 1848, after the Revolution, it was named College Colonial, and it was thirty years later that Indians were admitted without any distinction of caste or creed. It was managed mainly by the priests of the Foreign Mission (*pretres des Missions Etrangeres*); but in 1899, the College Colonial was laicised and became a secular school, also open to girls. After the Second World War, it is called College Français. In 1954, during the de facto transfer, it was in the courtyard of the College Français that Jawaharlal Nehru, pronounced his historic affirmation that 'Pondicherry should be a window of French culture', open towards France. Finally, in 1973, the College Français was designated as Lycee Français, borne by all the educational institutions in France which prepare students for the Baccalaureat. The nursery annexe was added in 1976, and last year, the Lycee Français obtained the buildings of the former French Cluny, which now houses the elementary section of the lycee. Around 1,500 students enroll in the Lycee Français nowadays. It also has an important *Centre de Documentation et d'Information* (C.D.I.) where about 20,000 books, magazines and newspapers enrich knowledge. Since 1992, a satellite antenna in the Lycee Français also receives the French television programmes. The Agence pour L'Enseignement

Français a L'Etranger (A.E.F.E.), created in 1990, ensures the smooth functioning of the Lycee Français in Puducherry.

The other organisation in India (Puducherry included) where teaching is effected through French alone is the Alliance Française. It was founded in 1883 by Pierre Foncin, a French geographer. It is a non-lucrative association which aims at propagating the French language and civilisation in a spirit of dialogue and exchange. Its present international network spreads to 130 countries as a French teaching centre with a view to promote culture. The fifteen Alliance Française in India form the most important network of Asia. In fact, more than 20,000 students learn French there, taught by around 200 professors. The Alliance Française in India also cooperates with the Indian Council for Cultural Relations (ICCR) to produce joint cultural events like concerts and dance shows, film retrospectives, itinerant exhibitions. Last year, the Alliances Françaises organised a competition of French songs. 'Operation French Nightingale', '*et l'on va chanter français en Inde*' ('and we are going to sing French in India'). The whole Indian network is coordinated in Delhi by a central institution called the 'Delegation Generale de l'Alliance Française en Inde', ensuring the cultural link between India and France.

So far the teaching of French in Puducherry is concerned, it is being done as a second language in the local schools. The colleges in Puducherry also offer BA (French Main) and MA French as graduation and post-graduation courses. French as a foreign language (FLE–*Français Langue Etrangere*) is taught at the local Alliance Française (started in 1889 in Pondicherry) or the Departments of French of the local colleges and the Pondicherry University (founded in 1986). The Kanchi Mamunivar Centre for the Post-Graduate Studies offers an MA French focusing on the French literary works, while the MA French at the university stresses on the theory and practice of translation and interpretation as well as on communication techniques, French language, literature, civilisation and culture over a span of four semesters where the student has to score seventy-two credits in this 'Choice Based Credit System' (CBCS). The Puducherry Community College, associated with the University, also offers a one-year Diploma in Functional French.

The Franco-Pondicherrians

The decree relating to personal status promulgated on 3 January, 1882 permitted Pondicherrians who wished to renounce their civil status as Hindus, Muslims or Christians to become 'French citizens', 'with the rights and duties which that entails.' Possibilities had been since that time open to those who renounced their civil status to pursue a career in the overseas civil service and in the army. The majority of the people who did renounce their status to become French citizens came from humble background and from low castes; though some came from high caste as well—for example, the Vallajas and Mudeliars. The former tended to embrace a military career which was easily accessible to them, whereas the Mudeliars, better educated and having a better knowledge of French, entered into the civil service, or specialised in liberal professions, law and medicine. A number of these civil servants and military personnel served in the French colonial territories, above all in Indo-China until 1954, the year of the defeat of Dien Bien Phu and of the de facto transfer of the Indian settlements which had remained French.

In 1962, day of the de jure transfer of Pondicherry, few Pondicherrians, a great majority of whom were those having renounced their status, chose the French nationality. Among them a large part were militaries stationed in Europe (Germany, France) or in Africa (Djibouti). These Frenchmen, often sons of militaries themselves (one can assume that, driven by the same reasons, their parents would also have made the same choice), hold a considerable position in the actual community, …A relatively small number of active civil servants also chose French citizenship… most often from high caste (Vellajas, Mudeliars)….' After 1962, one was again able to obtain French nationality (in the case of those who were registered), but after 1954, Franco-Pondicherrians could no longer enter the civil service which had become Indian. Only the military career remained easily accessible to them and those who enlisted, could therefore be from socio-culture and socio-professional milieu, which were probably more open than earlier. In the course of the survey, several Franco-Pondicherrians spontaneously mentioned these events which have remained determinant for their destiny.

6 Cultural and Spiritual Aspects of Puducherry

The Coromandel Coast

The Coromandel Coast rests on the east coast of India. Many European writers and trading companies have mentioned the east coast of India as Coromandel Coast in their official documents. However, the Portuguese were the first to apply the term *Charamandel* to the coast of the present day Tamil and Telugu states. Barbosa referred it as *Choromandel* as against the original printing of the term *Charamandel.* But the etymological root of Coromandel derives from the land of the Chola dynasty called *Cholamandalam* in Tamil, literally translated as the realm of the Cholas, which was later corrupted to Coromandel by the Europeans. The Coromandel Coast is also referred to as *Cholamandal Kadalkarai* (*Kadalkarai* means 'coast') in Tamil. But, it is referred to as *Kurumandel* along the eastern coast of the erstwhile state of Madras which comprised Kanchipuram, Kaveripattanam and Tanjore districts on the Kuru-Mandal coast of Kodikarai or Kodiyakkarai.

The Portuguese looked upon the entire Tamil coast as forming two trading regions. One region called Costa da Pescaria extended from the area south of Adirampattinam up to Kanyakumuri and the other region known as Costa da Choromandela was the north Tamil coast. It should be noted here that Coromandel referred as a Choromandela in Portuguese was between the river basin of Swaranmukhi and Point Calimere (Kodikkarai) in the Bay of Bengal. Some researchers defined the cultural region for the Coromandel ranging from the river Mahanadi to Cape Comorin; or from Madras to Cape Comorin or from Palvetkadu to Vetaraniyam. However, it may be justifiable to define the Coromandel Coast geographically as ranging from river Mahanadi to Cape Comorin, because the etymological root of the term Coromandel is essentially connected with the time of the Chola kings. One of the three Tamil kings (Mooventharkal) ruled in Tamil Nadu with his empire covering the present Coromandel coastal area. It is attested by Bavinck's classification of the coastal areas of Tamil Nadu state into three categories—coastal areas from Pulicat Lake to Point Calimere called Coromandel, from Point Calimere to Rameswaram called Palk Strait and Rameswaram to Kanyakumari (Cape Comorin) called Gulf of Mannar.

The Coromandel fisherman

Puducherry has a long coastal area along the Bay of Bengal and is connected with the sea coast of Tamil Nadu. Puducherry has a large fishing community. They speak Tamil, but the speech differs from the standard variety of Tamil in terms of accent and vocabulary. Many words related to fishing as well as many culture related words can be observed. A brief account of the fishermen of Coromandal area is given below.

The Pattinavar

The term Pattinavar is also pronounced 'Pattanvar' by some local people (*pattinam* = 'seashore town'; *var* = 'people'—literal meaning a dweller in a town or *pattanam*, a word which occurs in the names of various towns on the sea-coast e.g. Nagapattanam or Nagapattinam, Veerampattanam or Veerampattinam). The people are an indigenous and predominant Tamil speaking fishing community inhabiting the coastal belt of the Coromandel coast of Tamil Nadu. The Coromandel coast geographically considered the areas from Pulicat Lake to Point Calimere. They share common socio-cultural practices over several centuries, yet exhibit distinctive features of religious beliefs and regional dialects at the village level.

The Pattinavar fisherfolk are considered as most backward by the government administrations whereas they refer to themselves as Chettiyar and feel their social status to be equal with other inland upper social class communities. They are an endogamous caste group and do not marry into other fishing castes namely Paravas, Parathavar, Mukkuvar and Karaiyar who inhabit the coastal areas of Tamil Nadu. Pattinavars are divided into two endogamous sub-castes namely Cinna Pattinavar, and Periya Pattnavar. There is an ethnohistorical cause behind this sub-caste classification.

Pattinavars are Saivites (Hindus), but also worship various gods and *grama devatas* (village or clan deities). In some places, they regard Kuttiyandavar or Kanniyamman as their sea gods. Pattinavars generally speak Tamil but they have regional dialects. Even though the caste council referred panchayat declines among inland caste groups, Pattinavars still practice this type of caste council to solve their problems related to fishing activities, family and community.

A few vocabulary items which are characteristics of Pattinavar speech have been given below with their meanings in English.

Tatta	mother's (younger) sister
Valaikku pooyiRRan	has gone for fishing
Metappaa teriyum	approach of fish is observable
paaDu onRum sariyille	netting of fish is not good
kaDaara pooyiRRaar	has gone to the seashore
saangiyam	rituals
sikaram poyiRRaar	has gone to in-laws's house

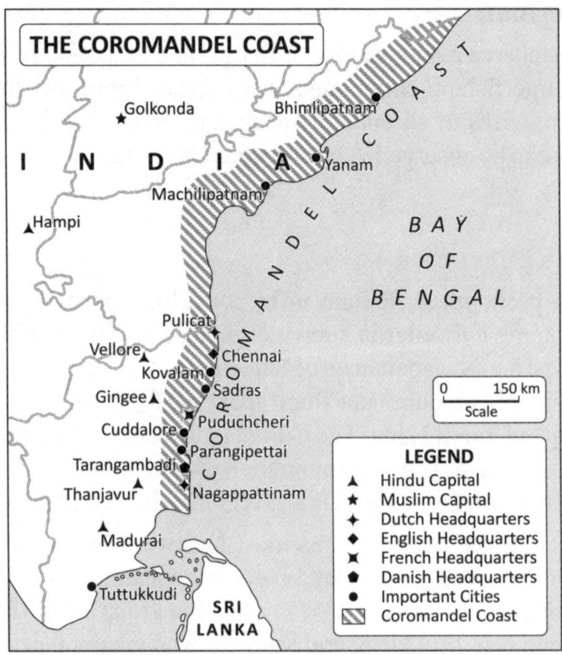

FIGURE 6.1: THE COROMANDEL COAST

AUROVILLE AND THE SRI AUROBINDO ASHRAM

Auroville

Auroville is located in Tamil Nadu but some parts of Puducherry are also covered, a few kilometers inland from the Coromandel Coast. Auroville is a universal township in the making for the population of 50,000 people from across the world. As early as 1930, the Mother decided that an ideal township devoted to human unity ought to be established. With her blessings and the initiative taken by the Sri Aurobindo Society in Pondicherry this concept of the Mother was put before the government of India. The government backed this proposal and took it to UNESCO. In 1966, UNESCO's General Assembly felt it as an important project for the future of humanity and passed a unanimous resolution. Subsequently, on 28 February 1968, some 5,000 people assembled near the banyan tree at the centre of the future township for an inauguration ceremony. It was attended by representatives of 124 countries and all the states of the Indian Union. The unique aspect at that ceremony was that each representative brought with them a handful of soil from their homeland, to be mixed in a white marble—lotus shaped urn which is presently placed at the focal point of the amphitheatre. At the same time Mother gave Auroville its Charter.

The Sri Aurobindo Ashram (SAA) counts some 1200 members; the Sri Aurobindo Society comprises 300 centres, fifty branches and includes 10,000 members in India and all over the world. In 1992, Auroville comprised 800 members of twenty-seven different nationalities, and a network of some ten centres in Europe (of which one is in Russia) and the United States. In 1997, the French and francophone community in Auroville comprised roughly 400 persons, which is 33% of the total population of Auroville.

The Auroville township project should not be confused with the Sri Aurobindo Ashram in Puducherry which is an entirely separate entity. Because of their shared aspirations both keep a very close relationship with each other.

Why Auroville?

The prime purpose of Auroville is to cherish human unity in its diversity. From this point of view, Auroville is the first and only internationally endorsed ongoing experiment in human unity. The population, the so called 'Aurovillians', have come from forty countries from all social classes, backgrounds, cultures, and age groups, thus representing humanity as a whole. The current strength of the population is 2,000 and is steadily growing. There are a number of schools providing education up to pre-college level. No examinations are conducted in most Auroville schools and no certificates are given. The New Era Secondary School follows a new national curriculum. Education is generally considered here as the means of giving impetus to each child's potential and freedom and opportunity to pursue his/her own individual path of growth and progress.

The Language in use in Auroville

Generally, English is the common spoken and written language of Auroville. Many people communicate in Tamil, French and other major European languages. Classes in English, French, Tamil, Sanskrit and Hindi are conducted mainly through language laboratory. In all the schools in Auroville, Tamil is invariably taught and classes are taken for adults who are interested in learning Tamil.

Auroville culture

Being located in the state of Tamil Nadu, Auroville supports Tamil culture. It has established a 'Centre for Tamil Heritage and Culture'. There are two more centres viz., 'Kuilapalayam Cultural Centre' and 'Mohanam Cultural Centre' in addition to Aranya settlement. In these places Tamil festivals are celebrated and classes are held for learning Tamil.

Sri Aurobindo Ashram

Founded in 1926, the Sri Aurobindo Ashram has grown, under the Mother's guidance, from a small group of two dozen disciples into a large diversified community with almost 1200 members. Counting the 400 students of the Centre of Education and the hundreds of devotees who live nearby, the larger ashram community consists of more than 2000 people.

The Ashram, located in the eastern part of Puducherry on rue de la Marine, is one of the most well known ashrams in India, with devotees from India and all over the world flocking to it for spiritual salvation. Its spiritual tenets represent a synthesis of yoga and modern science. It is open to the public daily between 08–1200 hrs and 1400–1800 hrs. Children below three years of age are not allowed into the ashram without the permission of the ashram authorities. Situated in a busy city of 7,89,416 people, the ashram is not a quiet place of retreat but a vibrant centre of life. The dynamic character of the community reflects the life affirming aim of Sri Aurobindo's yoga. Work as an offering to the Divine is an essential aspect of yoga, and all Ashramites do a certain amount of productive work each day in one or another of the Ashram's departments.

In the *sadhana* or spiritual discipline at the Ashram, there are no obligatory practices, no rituals, no compulsory meditations or systematic instructions in yoga. *Sadhaks* (ashramites) are left free to determine the course and pace of their *sadhana* in accordance with their own natures. But the general principle of the *sadhana* is the same for all: there must be surrender to the Divine and an opening to the Divine Force so that it may work to transform one's being.

Ashramites live and work in a large number of buildings spread throughout the area of the Ashram. The focus of community life is the Ashram main building, usually called simply 'the Ashram', which consists of an interconnected block of houses, including those in which Sri Aurobindo and the Mother lived for most of their lives. At its centre, in a tree-shaded courtyard, lies the *Samadhi*, a white marble shrine where their bodies are laid to rest.

The Ashram provides its members with all they need for a decent and healthy life. Various departments have been organised to look after the basic requirements of food, clothing, shelter, medical care. There are also libraries for study and facilities for a variety of cultural pursuits. The Ashram is administered by the Sri Aurobindo Ashram Trust.

FIGURE 6.2: A VIEW OF THE SRI AUROBINDO ASHRAM

Index